YOU CAN'T MAKE THIS UP

FIFTY-EIGHT YEARS AS A COUNTRY VET

RUSSEL HUNTER DVM

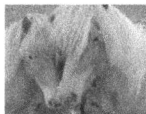

Tillasana Publishers, 42493 Hillcrest Loop, Astoria, Oregon 97103, rlhdvm@gmail.com

❀ Created with Vellum

This book is dedicated to my father, Robert Hunter.

ACKNOWLEDGMENTS

I have been assisted by some wonderful friends with extraordinary literary talents.

Thank you Julie Brown, Barbara Hansel and Mandy Schimelpfenig for your thoughtful ideas and encouragement.

Thank you Jan Johnson for guiding me from taking the written word and moving it into a book.

And finally, thank you Molly for carefully reading my stories. It's something I could never do.

INTRODUCTION

I've been collecting these stories for years. Then I started telling them. Now I'm writing them down.

They come from almost 60 years of being a country vet driving around countless back roads caring for farm animals. Some even come from earlier times as a student, or before.

They are all stories of irony.

Many are humorous, but certainly not all. Some attest to our ability to solve problems in almost impossible situations. Some have sadness in them. Some have a deeper, if unclear, meaning. Certainly, many result in closer and deeper friendships.

These are all true stories. That said, I might have changed some of the facts and maybe some names too, although many of the people have been dead for years and years.

CALIFORNIA

1

Beginnings

IT'S a bit fuzzy at this point, my beginnings with large animals and later becoming a veterinarian.

I think it sort of happened like this. This is where the interest started. Particularly in bigger animals. This was a really big animal— one I did not even see. Maybe.

I grew up at the edge of a small town in California. We walked to school every day past some houses, through some small fields. Everybody walked then.

Down the road, not too far in a large unused field, the circus would come. Almost every year too. My family was too poor to buy tickets, so we would watch the circus set up its tents and move the animals from their trucks into pens. That was a pretty good show right there.

One year the circus came near the end of the school

year, maybe May. I was around 9 years old, probably in third grade.

We were about to go home one afternoon when a note was given to our teacher. In those days there was no intercom, no telephone in the classroom and a half a century away from the cellphone. My teacher read the note with some concern and then announced it to us.

"Be careful when you go home," she told us. "An elephant has escaped from the circus, and nobody knows where it is." Looking back, she seemed pretty casual about the whole thing.

It wasn't casual to us kids. Not at all.

Everyone of us was immediately thinking that an elephant escaped from the circus, nobody knew where it was, and we kids are supposed to walk home. Walk home now with an elephant on the loose. We were truly freaked out.

We couldn't call our mothers either. Well, we could, but that wouldn't help. They wouldn't have a car to drive because all of our fathers drove off to work, somewhere, every day. Plus many of our mothers didn't even know how to drive.

We were on our own.

I had two friends that I usually walked with. We lived near each other.

Two or three is always braver that one, so off we went. We would move very cautiously. We would very, very carefully approach an intersection. All would search for an elephant, then run across the road and hide in bushes around a nearby house. We would move house to house in the bushes. Open fields were really scary as we were totally exposed. But we did it, it was the only way home. Anyway, we didn't have any choice.

Finally we made it home, safely. No elephant sighting either.

Later the escaped pachyderm was discovered in a nearby backyard drinking from a fishpond.

So, it all started by not finding a very large animal.

2

Feeding Yourself as a Student

THERE WERE two things about vet school.

One, it was hard and took a lot of time. We were in classes all day long, sometimes Saturday and we had to help with night calls too.

Two, we were poor. Maybe we got a little family help, but usually not much. We had to earn our way through school. Summers were good for making money, but that was never enough. So most of us worked some during the school year, usually part time and on and off. We couldn't work too much or it would interfere with our college studies.

We had to work out survival techniques.

Phil and I rented a small cottage. It had a kitchen, bathroom and common room for everything else including bunk beds. Not many people would live in it today. It was marginal at best. Monthly rent was $45. We split it.

We had never lived on our own before and didn't know how much food would cost or how much to spend. In a flash of brilliance, we decided to spend $45 monthly, and of course, split it.

After several months, we had to face the fact that $45 monthly was just not enough. It would only feed us 6 out of 7 days a week.

But we were poor. This was a dilemma.

Fortunately, with another flash of brilliance we came up with a solution. On the seventh day we would mooch off our girlfriends. This worked out especially good for me. Mine was an excellent cook and eventually became my wife.

This was an agricultural college, and it had a farm attached to it. The farm raised seemingly everything, but for research. There was a lot of food out there, although it wasn't for the public or even poor students.

We concluded there was plenty of extra food on the college farm, more than was really needed for research, so we devised a plan to harvest some of the abundance.

This took three poor and hungry students. Each had an assigned task.

One was for surveillance or looking out for the college cops. This was essential for our success, nutritionally and legally.

One was for harvesting. Strawberries were one of our favorites and there were some wonderful varieties being grown. Tomatoes were always good too.

The last person had a notebook and wrote fictitious information about the research we were supposedly helping with. That was a cover in case our surveillance failed.

We didn't keep at this very long. Not that we ever got caught. We didn't. We were scientists at heart and eventually felt guilty about disrupting a research project. The strawberries were great, however.

One summer I worked on the poultry farm on campus. Truthfully, it was a pretty lousy job: feeding all sorts of chickens, cleaning up after them and helping with research projects. Lousy job, but I needed the money.

One of the professors had a strange genetic research project.

She had come across a group of chickens that had very few feathers. A few around the lower legs, some on the wings and around the head too. She was breeding them and studying something. These birds were very, very ugly. Without feathers they sunburned and often turned purple.

After these chickens had performed their research duties, whatever that might have been, they were removed to a cull pen. Birds in the cull pen were eventually sold or terminated.

A cull pen for a poor student is a good food source, regardless of what's in it. The naked chickens, as they were called, were big and fleshy. Lots of meat, but very ugly. I found that if I skinned them, they looked like any other chicken. I just had to make sure nobody saw the bird before it was skinned.

They tasted fine as long as you didn't think about it too much.

3

My Starling Project

WHEN YOU'RE GOING to college you take on a lot of strange jobs to earn money. One summer, I worked for a professor who received a grant to attempt to find a biological control for Starlings. Yes, the bird.

Starlings are not native to North America. They were apparently introduced several hundred years ago from England. Since then, they have spread rapidly across the continent. They are very intelligent, adaptable, gregarious and aggressive. And they can successfully compete with native birds. Another problem was the damage they caused to agriculture, especially fruits. At this point they were considered pests. Really bad pests.

My professor had come across a virus he wanted to use as a biological control. It was a pox virus that caused growths around the bills. Only Starlings were affected, fortunately.

He surmised I could infect a group of Starlings, harvest the biggest and worst growths and pass them on to another batch of birds. Eventually I could find a strain of the pox virus that would be fatal. Then a biological control would be available. There was a Starling trapping system at the college in the farm area, so a supply of birds was never in doubt.

So I commenced with my research project. I would select the worst pox, harvest them, grind them up and reinfect another batch of birds. Maybe a dozen at a time. It would take 10-14 days to get a new batch of pox growths.

I carried this project out all summer. Infecting birds, harvesting the biggest and worst pox growths and passing them on, time and time again. Slowly, I was developing a more and more potent virus.

Finally, near the end of the summer, I had produced a very potent virus. All the birds were severely infected. It was so potent their bills would fall off.

There was a problem, however. A serious problem. This virus had no impact on the birds. They went about their business of living, which was largely eating, even with their bills missing. Eventually, they recovered, their bills grew back, and they were normal birds again.

Watching this happen was certainly astonishing and although I certainly realized these birds were pests, it did give me great respect for Starlings and their survival abilities.

By the way, we terminated the research after that discovery.

4

Work

IT STARTS EVERYDAY with the phone ringing. Hopefully, it's not too early. Hopefully the sun is up and it's light, I'm up, showered, dressed and most importantly, had some coffee. Definitely coffee, that's most important part.

I ask some questions, take some notes and try to figure where to fit this problem in. Is it an emergency, or something that can wait, maybe hours, or a day or two? Plus, I have lots of country to cover, lots of country. And I can't cover it all in a day, or even a day and a night. So I try to work areas as much as possible.

Most of the time I drive a pickup truck with a canopy in back to protect from the weather. It's usually rainy here. I built a special box from plywood for the back. It's got all kinds of drawers to hold all my needs: drugs, vaccine, stethoscope, thermometers, ophthalmoscope, hoof tools, long plastic gloves, surgery gloves, lots of surgical tools, coveralls, rubber boots, all kinds of ropes and restraint devices, assorted chemicals, endless syringes and needles, IV tubing. Probably a lot more.

So down the road I go. Maybe it's something very routine, like vaccinating a horse.

Or maybe it's more complex, like trying to figure why the cow is sick. In these cases, I ask questions and just watch the animal for a bit. Behavior has a lot to say. Then I will examine, maybe take blood or some other sample to examine later in my lab. At that point, I make some kind of a diagnosis. If we're lucky, a specific diagnosis and then a treatment, or maybe a surgery. If not, I try to come close to the problem, do the lab work later and come up with a solution.

Or maybe it's a horse with a bad leg that may require my x-ray to really figure out the problem. In the early days I had to develop the x-rays back in the office but recently I have a digital x-ray and can see them pretty much instantly. I can take as many x-rays as I want, too. That's really important in order to get the image just right. Anyway, horses don't always stand still.

Maybe next is a mare that needs to be examined for breeding. She needs an ultrasound exam, transrectal as they call it. That's where my long shoulder length plastic gloves become essential. I can examine the ovaries, measure things too.

Ultrasounds can give all kinds of information about organs, like x-rays can about bones. Ultrasounds have really changed over the years. The first portable one I had was so large that it had to be carried around in a wheelbarrow. But now the commonly used ones the size of a laptop computer with a probe connected by a cord. I even have one the size of my cellphone that sends the information to my cellphone. Who would have guessed?

Horses get injured often. They are emotional animals with thin skin especially compared to a cow. I need to look at one. It apparently ran through a barbed wire fence several days ago. The wound's infected and will take some special care. It will be alright, eventually.

Next, and hopefully last, I'm visiting a ranch. The owner has some concerns and drives me through the ranch. I'm looking over what might be behind his worries. After quite some time, I realize that I will need to return to collect blood and manure samples from his cattle and take grass samples too.

Then, if I'm lucky, I'm driving home. I'm thinking about the things I've seen and done. Maybe thinking about what I could have done better next time.

But, mainly, I'm thinking, or hoping I did some good and that I helped some animals and helped some people too.

5

He Don't Know

I WAS JUST fresh out of school and going to my see first sick cow. I was going to do this right and get off to a great start and impress the farmer.

Edward had his cow locked up along the road in a makeshift wooden head restraint. She stood there waiting looking rather subdued.

He was waiting too, probably wondering what the vet clinic sent him for a vet.

I needed to get some history.

"She had a calf two to three weeks ago. Even though she's a Jersey milk cow, I use her to raise orphan calves. Pretty good milker, just look at the milk bag, would you! Anyway, she's slowing down and not eating well and I'm worried. I hope you can figure it out and get her well."

I examined the cow thoroughly and finally arrived at her

problem. Basically, she was making so much milk she couldn't eat enough of the lousy hay she was being fed to make that amount of milk. So, she was stealing from her own body to make up the difference. Now she was getting sick from the imbalance. It's really a cow thing and how they process things internally.

But it's complicated to explain.

I tried though, and carefully laid it all out in rather scientific terms, like I learned at school.

Edward just nodded.

I went back to my truck to gather my treatment, mainly an IV for her and follow up things he could give.

While I was mixing things up, his friend Burt arrived on his old tractor. He turned it off and hopped off to stand by Edward.

"What's wrong with your cow?"

Edward looked at me, looked away and then at the ground and then said, "He don't know."

After that, I spent a lot of effort and time translating my fancy medical and scientific language into words that everybody could understand.

6

G etting There

USUALLY, it was a pickup. More rarely an old station wagon or now it would be called a SUV. But mostly a pickup. In early years they were rough things to drive and ride in with a stick shift and two-wheel drive. At least you didn't worry about tying a cow to your truck and hurting the truck.

The new trucks are different, completely different: automatic transmission, four-wheel drive and comfortable with a good heater, good air conditioning and windshield wipers that always worked.

But there were other ways of getting there.

It was later in the summer, near fall, when the calves would be bigger and ready to vaccinate. My boss, Dr Douglas, said, "Russ, I need you to vaccinate heifers at the Ingersol Ranch. There's about 70 head and they need Bangs." That was a mandated vaccine that only veterinarians could give. It was part of a big, nationwide eradication program against Brucellosis, a disease that infected cattle and humans.

I had never heard of this ranch before, but I agreed to do it. "Where are they, I've never heard of the ranch before?" I answered.

"It's a big ranch way out in the mountains. We only go there about once a year. It's too far to drive, Eddie will fly you out there."

Eddie was a retired vet with a small, very small airplane, but he had lots of flying experience. Anyway, he was still alive as an older man, so I thought that was encouraging. I was excited, but a bit apprehensive too.

"Meet him at the airport at 7 in the morning. It's going to take an hour to get there. Be sure to take everything you might need and some extra.

But you can't take too much, it's small plane."

I was edging more toward apprehension than excitement now, but that would get worse.

I met Eddie at 7 at the airport. We loaded up and there was barely enough room for the two of us and my gear. There were low clouds in the sky. "I'll fly under the clouds along the river until it clears. Then I can fly above the mountains. Where are we going?" he asked.

I was a bit surprised he didn't know, but answered, "The Ingersol Ranch."

"Not sure were that is, but I think it's way out there," he responded quite unconcerned.

"There are a lot of airstrips out there. We'll stop at one and ask." It seemed routine to him.

We flew along, got past the low clouds and climbed above the mountains. I was amazed by how big it all was. I could see ranches scattered about, airstrips too.

Finally, Eddie said, "Let's put the plane down at that airstrip and see if we can get some directions."

As we got closer you could see it wasn't much of an airstrip. There were rocks and debris scattered all over it. Eddie managed to land and avoid everything. He was trying to decide what to do next when suddenly a very old pickup came barreling toward us leaving a trail of dust behind. It stopped not very far away, and an older woman got out with a rifle pointed at us. "This is private property, get out right now."

"Sorry!" Eddie yelled at her, turned the plane around and we were airborne almost immediately. I was impressed, but then when an irate person is pointing a rifle at you, well you do things like that.

"That didn't work out very well," I finally said trying to break the mood.

"We still need directions," Eddie reminded me. He seemed unbothered by the experience.

We flew on past more ranches, then Eddie said, "Let's try that one."

I could see it looked different. This airstrip was kept up. There was even a plane at one end, and somebody was working on it.

Eddie landed us and taxied toward the plane at the far end. A man walked toward us wiping his hands clean of oil or grease. "Good morning, what can I help you with?" he asked. He was friendly and I began to feel relieved.

We told him where we wanted to go, and he helpfully and quickly gave us directions. "The landing can be tricky so give it a fly over before you land," he added.

We thanked him profusely and mentioned our last stop. He laughed and said, "That's old lady Forrester. You're lucky she didn't shoot your tires out, or worse."

We were off and it wasn't long before Eddie spotted the Ingersol Ranch.

He circled the airstrip once and then again. It was short, very short. The far end dropped off over a cliff. The windsock showed that we needed to land at the normal end and stop before going over the cliff.

Eddie took the plane down into the wind, but he landed too late. We were hurdling to the end of the strip and not slowing down fast enough.

Suddenly, when I figured we were about to go over, Eddie turned the plane sideways, and we skidded to a stop just at the cliff's edge.

Now we had to get to work and get the vaccinations done in record time. There was lots of good help, and the ranch had a great working system. I asked two of the ranch hands to help me. We needed to vaccinate, ear tag and ear tattoo each animal quickly so we could get back in the air and back to the coast before things clouded up.

We were back in the air in 60 minutes, barely time to say hello. However, the clouds had already moved in as we reached the coast.

"What's next?" I asked putting on brave front.

"I don't have radar, so I need to find a hole in the clouds and slip through it. Once we're under the clouds I can figure things out. Anyway, my gas is not going to last forever."

Let's face it, I wasn't having much fun at this point. I just wanted to get home and be on the ground.

Eddie flew us around for a while, long enough to make me wonder if we were going to run out of gas. Finally, he found a hole in the clouds. Quickly, he was down through, got his bearings, found the airport and we were on the ground.

That hole in the clouds was one of the most wonderful

things I have ever seen. I'll never forget it either.

7

Herd Work

IT's every young country vet's dream. Aspiration too. After one or two or maybe more years, you're pretty sure you're ready. You've been looking at a cow here, two there. A sick ewe. A horse or two all day long, it seems forever.

What you really want to do is look at a herd with a problem, one that's going to cause havoc or bankrupt the farmer. You want to figure out the problem and then come up with a solution.

Maybe it's a herd of cows and they're dying. You need to find out what's causing the deaths. Then you need a solution, a program to save the rest of the animals. It's pretty heroic, let's admit it, but it does a lot of good for the cows and the farmer. It makes you feel pretty good too.

One day my boss, Jack, said, "Issac's dairy has a milk

quality problem and the creamery wants it solved or they will quit buying his milk."

"Issac's dairy, I've never heard of it," I responded.

"We don't go there very much. Here's the address," he responded.

I called and made an appointment with Issac's wife.

A couple days later, on my way there I rehearsed what I would do: mainly examine the cows for infections and look over his sanitation procedures. Examining a lot of cows might take some time but maybe he had some records he could share with me to simplify and speed the process.

It took a while for me the find his place. It was on a back, unpaved road and it didn't look like a dairy. It barely looked like a farm.

There was a small house in front. It needed paint and other repairs, maybe a new front porch. The barn behind was unpainted and only two sided with a small milk room attached. "Pretty basic, or less," I thought driving up.

Issac was there waiting for me with his cows locked in individual stanchions. His milking herd. Three cows. Just three cows!

I stopped and got out of my truck unsure about what I was getting into.

Issac came to greet me, pleased I was now there. He was old, really old.

Little, wiry and spry. Happy I was there to help. He was easy to like.

I looked through his place first, milk room, cooling system. Everything was clean and neat.

The cows were next.

A cow has four mammary or milk producing glands. Each one is called a quarter and they are even more identified by location. Like left front, or right rear. With animals, if you stand at their back end looking towards the head, your left side is also their left side. Easy. Right.

I examined all three cows. That went pretty quick, well, because there were only three. The last cow had an infection in her right rear quarter and that was ruining his milk quality. Pretty simple as it turned out.

As I was explaining the problem and solution, I kept noticing that these cows looked really old. He was taking good care of them, but you can't cure old.

Finally, I asked, "These cows look pretty old. How old are they?"

"Oh, they're not old at all, maybe 13 or 14," he answered.

Actually, that's really old for milk cows, most are no longer around by eight or ten. Maybe even sooner.

Then he pointed to a cow behind the barn. I didn't see her before. She really looked old and had a big belly. "She's old, she's 24," he said.

He also told me she was due to have a calf in a month or so, so that explained her big belly.

It was a big day for me. I got to do some herd work and help the farmer. I also learned about cow longevity.

F inding the Needle in...

THIS WAS A LONG, long time ago. You could milk 30-40 cows and raise a family. Life was simple and cheap then.

Lars inherited his father's farm and barn as Lars's father had inherited from his father. The barn was redwood and would probably last forever. So would the land if you took care of it.

His cows were quiet, gentle Jerseys with large brown eyes. They came into the barn twice a day to be milked. Lars locked them in wooden stanchions for milking. They ate hay and maybe carrots while milked. The carrots depended on the season. If the weather was really bad, the cows stayed in the barn. The barn was poorly lit which could make things difficult for me at times.

Lars was Scandinavian, maybe Norwegian or Swedish. I'm not sure. He was older now and his once blond haired had grayed. At one time, he had been tall, but years of milking cows had stooped him. He was kind, gentle and quiet like his cows, except he had blue eyes.

He had a sick cow locked in his barn waiting for me. She had largely quit eating, was coughing and not making much milk.

It didn't take long for me to diagnose pneumonia. It would take several days of IV treatment to cure her.

I put a halter on her and pulled her head to her left and tied it in place to the next stanchion. This gave me access to her quite large jugular vein. This big vein runs in a groove near the front of the neck. If you push down on it, it distends above into a large turgid garden hose sized object.

The needles we use are very large, especially by human standards. This one was about 3 inches long and an 1/8 inch across. Because of the needle's size and the cow's thick skin, it takes quite a thrust to push the needle through the skin and into the vein.

It was a bit dark, and I had to bend over awkwardly. I pushed the vein closed with my thumb and thrust the needle into the cow and hopefully the jugular vein.

Then I looked, but didn't see the needle in the cow, or on the floor. I was confused.

Lars slid slowly to the floor and pointed at me. I wondered what he was he doing. I kept looking thinking I had seen the needle, only to have it disappear again.

Then I found it. I had missed the cow but slammed the needle through my thumb. I couldn't believe it. I had felt nothing.

Lars finally recovered enough to say, "Go to the hospital, forget about my cow."

I wasn't about to abandon his sick cow.

It still didn't hurt but pulling it out didn't look like much fun either. And I certainly couldn't ask Lars to help. He was taking all this much worse than I was.

I needed a pair of pliers which he reluctantly got me.

I had to study this for a bit in better light. Finally, I went outside where I could see better. I put the plier tips around the needle, held it steady. and jerked my hand away. That hurt, it really hurt but the needle was free. My thumb seemed alright considering what happened. It was probably doing better than Lars was.

I got another needle, successfully found the cow's jugular vein and gave her antibiotics. Furthermore, I repeated that treatment for 3 more days.

In the end the cow recovered. So did Lars. So did my thumb.

A
Shot in the Mouth

NORTON WAS A VERY UNPLEASANT MAN. Actually, that is quite an understatement, but I'm trying to avoid certain words in these stories.

He was mean, vindictive and cruel. Nobody wanted to be around him. I always hoped he did not have a family to suffer his ways.

He ran a few cows which he treated poorly. They were always skinny because he refused to feed them correctly. They lived in an enclosure made of old cars, pickup trucks, dump trucks and tractors. Bed springs too, they were the gates in and out.

I got assigned to take care of his cow problems because I was the new vet. I was told it was character building, but the truth was nobody could stand him.

He had a cow trying have a calf, but with no luck. He

had her caught in headlock when I arrived. She had been trying for some time without success. She had spent a lot of time straining hard.

I cleaned her up and examined her. She had a calf coming backwards, but the back legs were pointing frontwards. Just the tail was coming out. It's called a breech birth, and they need help.

These are not easy to correct.

After some time and effort, I was able to bring the back feet backward for delivery. It's tough work because the cow won't stop straining. Along with the straining comes projectile feces. I always stand as much to the side as possible to avoid getting drenched with manure.

I put chains around both back feet and handed Norton a handle to hook into the chain for pulling out the calf.

"Stand off to the side," I warned him.

He just sneered and stood directly behind the cow. We started pulling, the cow started straining. Just as the calf was ready come out, she let loose with a massive load of feces right into his mouth.

I turned to ask if he wanted to clean up.

He glared and said, "Keep pulling," while spitting out some of the manure.

We did, and the calf arrived alive. I quickly cleaned up and left happy to be out of there, happy there was a live calf and, probably happiest about his mouthful of manure.

It was a delightful drive home.

10

The Green Arm

I WAS MAKING a long circuit through the Northern California coastal mountains stopping at farms, ranches and even houses along the way.

There were no cell phones in those days and not everyone had a phone in their home. But enough did and there were always pay phones at gas stations, cafes and grocery stores. In those days, pay phones cost a dime to use.

By midafternoon I was able to contact my wife about incoming problems. She was home caring for our small kids and answering the phone.

Only one caller had phoned, but many times and my wife was exasperated trying to answer the concerns.

Beth had a horse with colic. That's a belly ache in a horse. Colic can be simple and self-curing, like gas we get from a Mexican dinner, or life threatening and fatal. It's always painful and horses are emotional animals, so they display their pain well.

I had been to Beth's before. It was a small farm near the top of a ridge with some horses and cattle wandering around. There was a lot of heavy equipment scattered around too. I wasn't sure how she made a living, maybe driving her trucks, CATs, backhoes and tractors for hire.

Now, Beth was a big, stout woman and nothing in life spooked her. Had I been inclined to get in bar fights, I definitely would want Beth for my back up.

I got there in about 30 minutes. As I drove up, I could see a horse tied to a dump truck. Big trucks have lots of uses. Behind the horse was a very large pile of horse manure.

Beth walked with her bare right arm extended covered with green horse manure.

"She's fine now. Your wife told me what to do".

I was dumbfounded. My wife would never tell somebody to stick their arm up a horse's rectum. It's too dangerous unless you know how to do it and can really trust the horse.

"What?" I said.

"I kept phoning her asking for any advice or help, anything. Finally, she told me she has seen you stick your arm in the rectum and remove manure."

Well, that was true. I do that, all vets do that. But it's done to remove the manure so we can examine the abdomen, the intestines and other tissues for abnormalities.

As it turned out, Beth's horse had a mild case of constipation. Her removal of the manure cured the horse. Now all she had to do was clean up her arm!

She was a brave and resourceful woman.

11

Captured by a Trestle

THE FAMILY LIVED along a small creek that over the years had carved out a tiny valley. They had fenced off their part and kept a few cows and an old family horse, a mare.

A rarely used railroad track ran through the property. Instead of dipping into the little valley, a trestle has been built to span it. It was quite old and built with huge timbers you would never see again. The sides of the trestle, the part that supported it and the trains the passed over it, were beams 30 inches deep and 6 inches wide. Enormous. Those kind of trees are long gone.

For years, the animals had grazed back and forth under the trestle without concerns.

One day the old mare was under the trestle grazing with her head down. For some reason raised her head. Maybe a sound startled her. All she could see were the enormous beans of wood supporting the trestle. She was trapped and scared. She had no idea how to escape.

Finally, the family found her, put a halter on her and tried to lead her out. She wouldn't budge. They brought grain, no luck. Apples, no luck. Carrots. Nothing worked.

They called and asked me to help. It seemed pretty simple to me, but it wasn't. I was no more successful than they were. And the more we tried the more frightened the mare became.

She would not lower her head to be led out.

After some thinking, I realized I could lower her head with a potent IV tranquilizer. She was easy to handle, I gave her the IV and waited. Finally, her head dropped, almost to the round. We got behind her and pushed. Slowly she staggered out and was free.

Running in Circles

LIVING in the mountains of Northern California and caring mainly for horses and cattle and sheep also meant I cared for an occasional dog. We were just too far away from dog and cat hospitals.

Bev was a big woman. A really big woman with a quite small dog. Maybe you've seen this before, but they like to carry them between their breasts. Nice shelter actually.

Bev was worried about her small terrier like dog. "He's acting super nervous. A bit nuts, actually."

Well, this was rabies country, and any strange behavior brought up the big red flag of maybe rabies. Such a terrifying and fatal disease. Contagious too.

She came to our small house in the woods. Her sister came too.

The dog was very, very, very excited.

To watch its behavior I asked her to put it on the ground. Immediately the dog started running in a circle about 10 feet across. After two or three laps I grabbed it as it came by.

I examined it as well as I could and began to think this wasn't rabies but something else. Maybe the dog ate something that caused this. Maybe it was poisoned.

In those years, it was common to use amphetamine type drugs for weight reduction in humans. Of course, this would be a sensitive subject to broach.

Finally, I did ask her if there were any prescription drugs the dog could have accidentally eaten.

The answer was a quick no. It was obvious she did not appreciate my question.

I needed to think about this. I had seen this before, so I didn't really believe her. As I put the dog down her sister approached and led me a little away.

"Bev is on diet pills and sometimes she spills them and the dog will eat anything."

That made sense to me and certainly calmed down my concern of rabies.

I finally told her that somehow her dog was poisoned and that I would sedate it and send sedation home until it returned to normal. And I suggested she be very careful about what the dog got into.

After a few days her dog was fine.

I don't think Bev's stature ever changed, but her dog always had a cozy spot.

13

The New Cattle Chute

THE SUTTER FAMILY had land along the coast not far from the ocean. They ran a herd of beef cattle, Herefords. Like many other folks they logged too.

Every fall, at weaning time, they separated the cows from their calves. Then they separated the steers from the heifers. In those days heifers were required to have official brucellosis vaccinations. That was my job. This was a disease that caused havoc in cattle and was contagious to humans. Many farmers, ranchers and vets in in the old days had contracted the disease. In humans it was called Undulant Fever. It was hard to get rid of once you got it too.

They had a lousy system for working the heifers and every year I threatened not to come back. It was slow and dangerous for the animals and the people.

When they called this time I hesitated, but they quickly

assured me they had built a new system, particularly a new chute with a squeeze.

I was elated and set up an appointment date.

When I arrived on the time and date we set up, I was happy to find they had a designed and built remarkable wooden cattle chute with even a squeeze. A squeeze helps restrain cattle even better.

We set right to work. They smaller heifers first, then larger ones and finally the largest ones.

Everything worked fine, in fact wonderfully. Then we got to the larger heifers. The first two were ok, but it was a tight fit. I was a getting bit worried.

With a lot of work, they finally got the third of the biggest heifers in the chute and locked in. I vaccinated her. That went ok. When we tried to release her, she was stuck.

We shoved, pushed, pulled and, of course, swore. No luck, she was stuck.

There was only one option, and it was a terrible one.

They had to completely take apart this beautifully designed and built wooden chute. I stayed to help them and make sure the heifer was ok when freed.

14

——————

S ick Ears

LOUIE HAD a small dairy in the big valley in California. He milked about 50 big, black and white Holstein cows.

But his life was about to change.

He had met Maria, they fell in love, and were soon to get married.

Maria worked for a insurance company in town and she was a city girl.

He decided to milk more cows to support the future family they already were talking about.

Louie bought 50 more cows. They soon started having calves and giving him milk. He convinced Maria to feed all the new calves. She was willing, even excited, but nervous. After all, she was a city girl and knew nothing about cows, let alone raising baby calves.

He showed her all the important things about raising calves.

However, Maria was concerned something could go wrong and the calves would get sick. She asked Louie about sick calves. He explained sick calves get droopy ears and you give penicillin injections until they get better.

"How will I know when they get well?" she asked.

"Simple," Louie replied, "When the ears go back up."

"OK," Maria thought, "I can do that."

Sometime later, Louie called me to visit his farm to look over some cows he was worried about.

I met Maria as I entered the barn to look at Louie's cows. She seemed to want to talk to me but was hesitant.

As I worked my way through the cows and answering Louie's questions, I noticed Maria hanging around the door to the barn.

Finally, when we finished, Louie turned to me and said Maria had some questions about her calves. I approached Maria and asked about her concerns.

"I have sick calves, and they don't get better."

I went through my standard questions.

"Do they eat?"

"Yes."

"Do they have diarrhea?"

"No."

"Cough, runny eyes?"

"No."

Finally, I asked why she thought they were sick.

"They have droopy ears. Louie told me to give them penicillin until the ears went back up, but their ears don't go back up and I'm worried."

"Let's go look," I said although I was a bit perplexed by her story.

The small calf barn was very tidy. Maria really took care of things. I could see that quickly.

The calves were in individual stalls in a row. As we entered the barn, all the calves poked their heads out the front of their little stalls. They were probably hoping for more milk.

And, yes, they all had droopy ears. Every one of them. They were black and white like their mothers. The new cows had been bred to a Brahma bull and all the calves had his droopy ears. Penicillin was not going change these ears!

Maria's great relief showed as I explained this to her.

15

W aiting for Luis

He had moved from Portugal to California, maybe 30 years ago.

Luis quickly found a job milking cows on a dairy in the big valley. He milked 20-30 cows twice daily, by hand. At night he had to soak his hands to stop the pain and swelling.

Soon he met a girl, they fell in love, got married and then worked together on the dairy. She fed calves and he continued milking.

They earned $40 monthly. They saved $35 of it. Yes, that's hard to believe, but that was 60 years ago. Times have changed.

Before many years, he bought some cows, then rented a place and then bought a place. Now he had his own dairy.

By the time I met him he owned a dairy and had many

cows. He no longer milked cows, he had help to do that. Furthermore, miking was now done with machines.

Now he had a cow unable to have her calf. She was in a large corral. I roped her, made a halter out of the lariat and tied her to the fence.

It didn't take long to figure out the calf was much too large for her to pass. A cesarean surgery would be needed.

This was not a good spot and there were just the two of us. However, there weren't any options at the moment. Actually, typical in my life.

I sedated the cow, but just lightly and we pulled her down with ropes and tied her upside to the fence. She was going to be a belly approach.

After I shaved the hair, cleaned the skin and injected a local anesthetic, I was ready to do the surgery.

"Are you ready?" I asked. I got a muted "Yes". Now I realize I should have been paying more attention to Luis.

I made a quick, large incision into the abdominal cavity. I was ready to cut into the uterus and remove the calf when I heard a sound and turned to find Luis face down in the dirt. He had fainted!

I stood there gloved up, scalpel in hand and ready to panic. "Luis," I yelled, "I need you, please."

Slowly he rolled over, cleaned himself up as much as he could and said apologetically, "I should have told, I can't stand blood."

"That's ok, but I need your help. Can you do it?"

"I'll try."

"Not much assurance," I thought, "but not much choice either."

I finished the surgery and Luis stayed with me to the end. We lost the calf, but the cow was fine.

16

Having Kids

HAVING kids hasn't really changed much in the last 50 years or so. That's when we had ours. What is different is paying for the kids. I'm talking about paying for their birth.

Our son was born well over 50 years ago in a small rural Catholic hospital. Wonderful nurses and doctor, although I was not allowed to watch the birth. There was something seemingly immoral about having a man in the birth room. Even the father.

After a long night of labor and hard work by my wife, our son was born. Normal too.

I was then off first thing that morning to examine a newborn foal. a colt. He was fine too. It was a good morning for birth.

To pay for the whole thing I sold my horse, Mike.

Although I had had him for several years, I really wasn't using him. I sold him to a young woman looking for a good horse.

$250 dollars for Mike. That covered the birth.

Although our son was healthy, he developed colic. New parents have a lot of trouble sorting out things even with normal babies, but the colic was just too much. We were quickly exhausted, especially driving country roads in the middle of the night to ease him into sleep. It was spring and I was putting in 12 hours or more every day.

After a week, we decided we needed help. We needed experience. The best experience we knew was my wife's mother. She should know everything about babies. She had raised 5 kids.

There was an airport not that far away, so she could fly to us easily. We decided and she flew up.

I met her at the small airport, took her to our home where my wife and son were waiting. Well, at least, my wife was waiting.

We sat her down in the living room and explained our dilemma. We needed her help to sort this out.

She was quiet for some time. Finally, she said, "You know that was a long time ago. I just don't remember what to do."

She did stay with us for quite a while helping around the house, cooking, cleaning. Those kinds of things. I could pay more attention to my busy workload too. Finally, everything got better. Maybe just having her around did it.

Three years later our daughter was born in another small, rural hospital. We had moved to a different area by then. We had a wonderful doctor, Dr. Phelps. He also had a cattle ranch. That worked out just fine for both of us.

He delivered our daughter. Once again, everything was normal. We were more experienced parents now and things went very smoothly.

I pregnancy tested his cows, did some vaccinations, looked at couple sick ones. We called it even. $500 for the birth.

17

Snake Medicine

"Doc, my wife's cow is off. She pretty much quit milking. She's nervous or scared about something. She won't eat much either. Ruth."

"Ruth?"

"That's the cow's name. My wife is Marilyn. She'll come to her name. Actually, both of them do." He chuckled. Northern California mountain humor.

Herb and his wife lived in the mountains east of the Eel River in Northern California along a county road. They had several acres with a small barn and a grazing area for the cow. Actually, it was Marilyn's cow. She was a sweet and very gentle Jersey that Marilyn just adored. Plus she gave delicious, rich milk. Marilyn made soft cheese and butter. Ice cream sometimes too. Maybe not that healthy, but delicious.

I looked over my schedule and realized I could swing by their place later the next morning.

"I'll stop by later tomorrow morning. Will anybody be around?"

"Nope, Marilyn works in town, and I'll be out driving my log truck until late. But she's tame, really tame and you can do anything with her. We'll leave a halter on her."

I don't usually like to handle cows alone, but I did know this one was very friendly. I told him I'd swing the next morning and check her out.

It was already warm by the time I arrived later the next morning. I stopped, got out of my truck and quickly spotted the cow. She was standing at the upper end of her little pasture. She looked uncomfortable, maybe even scared.

I always liked to observe animals before I catch them up and examine them. The grass had dried during the dry summer and was now brown. A warm morning sunbathed the area.

I called to her. She looked briefly at me but turned away and refused to move. I wasn't sure what to think.

The fence was sturdy and made of wood. Good for holding a cow and for climbing over. I walked to the fence, climbed over and stepped into her small brown pasture.

I grew up in rattlesnake county and long ago learned the sound of an angry snake. It's remarkable how quickly a ferocious rattle can send fear rushing through you. It says get away and fast, really fast. And it's amazing how fast you can move.

I was back over the fence and on the other side so quickly that I don't remember doing it.

When I looked back, I saw it, a six-foot rattlesnake that had claimed the area for morning sun. It was probably warming up after the cool nights we were starting to have.

Ruth, the cow, was now more distraught than ever. I'm sure that was last thing she wanted to hear.

Now remember, in those days there were no rattlesnake relocation services available. That's probably true even today in that country.

I walked back toward the house thinking about what I could do. Near the front porch, I found a shovel. "Aha," I thought!

I went back to the fence. The snake was still there, claiming it's spot. I crossed the fence away from the snake and dispatched it with the shovel.

I brought the snake back to the house and draped it over the front porch railing. Next to it I pinned a note that said, "Let's see if your cow doesn't get better."

She did.

18

The Snowstorm

CHARLEY HAD a ranch pretty high in the mountains. He lived alone and ran a herd of 100 mother cows. That doesn't sound like much today, but then you could make comfortable living. That's providing you drove your old pickup 20 years and had a tractor even older. Of course, a TV was out of the question and things like computers and cellphones were not even invented.

It was raining near the coast when I left to help him deliver a calf. Winter rain was normal there. Anyway, I was used to doing most cattle work in bad weather.

As I drove into the mountains and got higher and higher, it started sleeting. Then it turned to snow. Pretty soon everything was white. The snow was sticking now.

Charley was waiting for me in the house. He led me down to the corral just across the small county road. The cow was contained in a small pen. I put a rope on her, made it into a halter and started to work. She was quiet, probably tired from trying to have the calf. I soon decided this wasn't going to go easily or quickly. It was a big calf and not coming out straight.

It wasn't long before she gave up and lay down in the snow. I had to do likewise. It kept snowing, I kept working. This went on for a long time. The snow began to pile up and I had to push it away at times. Charley helped. I was getting colder too.

Finally, an hour later, we extracted the calf. It had not survived the ordeal. I wasn't doing much better either. The snow was now 6 inches deep, and I was really, really cold. My hands quit working.

Charley had to help me up. "Let's go to the house," I barely remember him saying to me. He helped me all the way. I was helpless.

In the house, I couldn't do anything. My hands didn't work. I was stuck in place. Carefully, Charley took off all my clothes, wrapped me in a blanket, and set me in front of his fireplace. He disappeared with my clothes but soon returned with a hot drink and some food. Hot chocolate and beef jerky.

Slowly, I warmed and drank hot chocolate and ate jerky. My hands went through that terrible burning when thawing out and then were better. Finally, I was warming. That took an hour, the same length it took to almost freeze me.

Charley brought my clothes, not quite dry, but warm. I was able to dress myself. He took my keys and brought my pickup near the house with the heater turned up as high as possible.

By the time I got home, I was warm and my clothes dry.

The rain seemed wonderful.

19

R ecalcitrant Uterus

NATURALLY, it was Friday night.

Bob called and he had a young Jersey cow that pushed her uterus out after calving. Well, that's a disaster that needs taken care of soon and takes people to do. He couldn't be there because his daughter had a basketball game. His help was probably gone, after all it was Friday evening. My wife assured me quite quickly, she had a school activity where she taught.

I finally said I would take a look and see what could be done. Maybe some help was still around, if I was lucky.

When arrived, I found her in a small area where they took care of cows that had just had calves. Nobody was around.

She was locked in a stanchion and casually eating hay

like nothing had happened. She had been hosed clean. Her uterus hung halfway to the floor!

Fortunately, she was small, really small. "Well, maybe I can do this," I thought shifting quickly to the heroic mode which often tramples sound thinking.

I tied her tail out of the way with some twine, got geared up with rubber boots and rain pants, cleaned her and laid out my needed supplies nearby.

Lastly, I put on shoulder length plastic gloves, secured them, and went to work.

As it turned out, I was able to replace the uterus pretty easily.

With my gloved arm, I followed it down into the cow until it was returned to where it belonged. I was pretty proud of myself, maybe a bit cocky at that point.

I removed my arm and turned to my supplies to get a hormone injection to contract the uterus quickly and hopefully stop it from being pushed out again. It needed to be given IV for fast results.

As I was filling the syringe, I heard a sound, turned around and found the uterus hanging out again. The cow remained unconcerned and was still eating hay. This was not good.

Again, I replaced the uterus and again the cow pushed it out. In fact, it happened two more times.

I looked around the place again, no help. I wasn't feeling so cocky anymore either, but this this couldn't go on without a real tragedy emerging.

I looked the cow over carefully and realized her two large milk veins, one on each side on her belly, were reachable from behind. She was little and that made this possible.

Then I filled my syringe with the hormone, held it in my

mouth and preceded to replace the uterus again. Again, I was able to it do fairly easily. With my hand still in the returned uterus and up to my armpit, I took the syringe out of my mouth, reached down and forward and made an injection into one of her large milk veins. The uterus began to contract almost immediately. As it contracted. I slowly brought out my hand. Contracted, the uterus was unable be expelled again. Whew!

It worked and the uterus stayed in place.

I still don't know who won the basketball game.

20

V et Kids

IT WASN'T long before my son started riding with me going to see sick animals in the country. He was, maybe, two or three. I wasn't going to have time to change diapers, so he had to be past that stage. My daughter was three years younger, so it it was a while before she started traveling with me.

At first, it's an adventure. Getting out of the house, seeing something new and different: places, people, animals and watching what I was doing.

Later, both kids narrowed it down. The vet call had to be really interesting or they had friends at the place or maybe a horse to ride. My daughter preferred a horse, my son a surgery or necropsy.

Eventually, they both got fairly well educated in life:

birth, disease, dying and death. And of course, reproduc-
tion. But that's also true with most farm kids.

They collected objects too, sometimes objects I didn't
even know about. These would sometimes end up at school
and be shown to the class at show-and-tell times the
teachers would conduct. It wasn't long before their principal
sent us a letter requesting our kids no longer bring things
for show-and-tell.

Once, before that note was sent home, I was called out to
determine why a mare had died rather suddenly. I
performed a necropsy, which is where a vet cuts open an
animal to figure out the cause of death. Owners may want
this done out of just plain curiosity. Usually, though, they
want to know so they can prevent it from happening again
or it spreading to their other animals.

As it was, this mare died of a strangled intestine. She was
about two months pregnant, so I removed the fetus to show
the owner and my son. It was a perfectly proportioned
miniature horse. I took it home and saved it in a small clear
jar filed with a preservative. I wanted to use it for lectures I
would give in the future.

As it turned out, my son took it to school for show-and-
tell. This was before the banning occurred. It was quite the
hit until one of the kids asked how it got inside the mare. At
that point my son was only too happy and willing to explain
horse breeding to his class. Of course, he had seen this in
the field on calls with me. Before the teacher could stop
him, he had pretty much graphically explained how it all
happens.

Hence, the note from the principal.

.   .   .

SOMETIME LATER WHILE riding with me after a day on farms and ranches, he asked how long a human baby in its mother. I answered, "Nine months, same as a cow." Probably a typical vet answer.

For a while he was busy with his fingers and thinking hard.

Finally, he said, "My birthday is in May, that means for me, you bred Mom in August."

Yep!

OREGON

21

M r. Brown

MONTE MILKED cows long enough to build some equity. They were Jersey cows and he lived in the big valley in California. He sold the equity, bought land in northern Oregon along the Columbia River, built a dairy barn and milking parlor and moved north with his cows.

It was a long move and a very big change in weather. His cows started getting sick. He called and offered to fly me north to look at his cows.

I was sort of between jobs, wandering around the northern California mountains trying to support a young family. We were good friends and anyway, there weren't any vets available to help him.

I caught a flight out of Eureka and puddle jumped my way north to Astoria in a small turboprop airplane. Coos

Bay, Lincoln City and finally Astoria. Once, we couldn't land because of a herd of elk on the runway and had to circle until they were chased off.

It was a November afternoon, getting dark. It was cold, windy and the rain was coming sideways. "Not sure about this," I thought.

Monte was waiting with his pickup. We drove from the airport east through Astoria and along the Columbia River. By now it was dark and still really stormy.

"Let's eat," he said and suddenly pulled up to a small cafe in a little town not far from his dairy.

This was going to be a hamburger and milkshake meal. I knew what he liked but that was fine with me.

The little cafe was really one U-shaped counter that looped back to the kitchen. We soon ordered and were waiting for our food. There were a few people there, mainly for coffee.

Suddenly, the front door opened and in shuffled a small, very old man wearing a rain hat and large trench coat. He sat down and took off his hat. Immediately, the waitress brought him a large cup of coffee about two thirds full. I know because he was sitting next to me, and I could see everything.

Obviously, he was a regular costumer.

He filled the cup with sugar and cream, mixed it and took a taste. Satisfied, he put it down and reached into his trench coat. He pulled out an opened can of dog food with a spoon in it and proceeded to have dinner.

He finished before we did and left, after all he only had part of a can of dog food. I learned later he was Mr. Brown and lived not far down the road in a remodeled chicken coop.

I had a lot of things to think about: this could be a harsh country, just look at the weather outside, but there was another side I realized as I watched the waitress take care of Mr. Brown.

Shortly, I moved north with my family. It's been over fifty years now.

22

————

H alting a Salmon Run

IT WAS a young and very ill horse that was losing weight, not eating well and quite weak. I put it in a small pasture next to my barn and along a small river. I made, at least, a partial diagnosis and started a course of treatment.

This was years go, and we didn't have the tools and drugs to work with that are around today. It was a long shot, but worth a try. Anyway, a good pasture was like chicken noodle soup for a sick horse.

It was a small pasture, fenced on three sides with a small river on the backside. There was a steep, brushy bank to the water, so it acted like a fence. Although it was fall, the grass was still lush and green.

It seemed like perfect place for a sick horse to get well.

The little river hosted a salmon run in the early fall. The

fish were Chinook or King salmon. They could be large, 10, 15, 20 even 25 pounds. Long too. Two to three feet long.

After a long dry simmer, the water levels were surprisingly low especially for big fish to navigate. The salmon seemingly always managed to find a deep enough spot to wiggle through. I was always surprised, however.

Late one afternoon, we returned after a day of caring for distant farm animals. I had my vet assistant Dan with me. I sent him out to catch the horse for an evening treatment. He returned empty handed.

"I can't find the horse," he told me.

We could see the fence was intact. The only other way out was the small river. That was not a good option and worrisome. We went searching.

We found the sick horse in the water, in the river. In fact, it was lying down in the river. More than that, it was lying in the only deep channel the salmon could swim through.

When we looked carefully, we could see a dozen or more salmon downriver. They were blocked and had nowhere to go. The horse was blocking the salmon run! This could be a real disaster. Probably illegal too.

We waded out into the water and after much struggling got the horse up. After more struggling, we got the horse out of the little river and up the opposite and gradual bank.

Slowly, we walked to horse back and across a small bridge to my place. It took both of us, as he was pretty weak.

After that we kept him in a safer pasture with no river access. He got better slowly, and the salmon continued their spawning run unobstructed.

23

A Belated Thank You

No names this time.

This story has some hard and ugly parts to it that I will not explain, but there is redemption and finally a thank you.

He had spent time in prison. Maybe a decade. The crime was ugly, despicable actually, but he came back to our community, probably scarred but determined to make a life. I commend him for that and he was largely successful too.

Soon he had a wife, property and a small herd of cattle. That's how I came to know him, taking care of his cattle. It was a scraggly backyard herd, but he raised food for the family and made a few bucks on the side.

I was always good to him, understanding the past and its difficulties. I've always believed in second chances. In turn, he was good to me and in ways I never realized. Not for years.

There were three boys too. They got relegated to the grandparents which was probably a godsend. They did as well as they could with the boys. There were limitations and certainly failures. Young boys need a father and they really didn't have one for maybe ten years.

As a consequence, the boys became the local pillagers. Nothing was safe. This was a concern, a great concern, to me. I had an office full of drugs and medical equipment, and a barn that could really never be closed up.

But it never happened. I was never robbed or vandalized. I was certainly mystified, but pleased too.

Now looking back, I'm pretty sure they received very explicit instructions to stay away from my place. I was taking care of the cattle that were providing all of them with food and their father with some income.

It took me years to figure this out and even more years to find him again give him a special thank you.

24

A Barrel of Baseballs

MR. HAGLUND LIVED with his wife along the county road near me. They were both retired. He had several acres of apple trees and pasture where they kept a couple cows and their calves. He raised new calves every year to sell in the fall.

Along the north side of his property was the Little League field.

This had become a source of contention for Mr Haglund. He was naturally grumpy, but Little League kids and their games drove him crazy. The kids were noisy and their parents even noisier. The kids were always running around. He just didn't like any of it.

But the worst were the baseballs that landed in his property. The foul balls.

He built a high fence and wouldn't let the ballplayers

retrieve any of the foul balls. Or the parents. Or the coaches. This had gone on for years now. He kept all the foul balls.

It was early fall, and a windy rainstorm has passed through a couple days earlier. That was typical for fall, one good windy rain that announced winter was coming.

Mr Haglund called me. He had a sick cow. It wasn't hard to figure out the problem. There were apples all over the ground and the cattle were eating them. The wind had blown them down. The sick one was the boss cow, and she had naturally eaten the most.

He had her locked in the barn. After clarifying the problem, I started treating her apple indigestion problem. This took some oral and intravenous medications. I told him I would need to return for a couple more days to get the cow well. He was a bit of a curmudgeon and wasn't looking forward to spending much money, but he didn't want his cow to die either.

I returned the next day and saw the cow was already better. She wasn't normal, but definitely better. I retreated her.

As I was walking through the barn, I noticed an open barrel. When I looked inside, I saw it contained baseballs. At least 200, maybe a lot more than that.

I asked him about them. He said they were foul balls that had landed on his property. He wasn't going to give them back as now they were his. I let it go and said nothing more.

By the third day, the cow was doing very well and wouldn't need further care after this. I treated the cow a final time. As I was putting things back in my truck, he came up with his check book and asked what he owned. He might had been a grump, but he paid his bills.

I had already thought about this and said, "I want the baseballs for payment, all of them."

He couldn't believe it. It was like he got everything I did free. Of course, that was true.

"You can't have the barrel, I need that," he replied. I didn't want the barrel anyway, so that was fine.

"No problem, how about some old feed sacks to put the baseballs in?"

We loaded several feed sacks with baseballs. I put them in the passenger side of my truck and left.

I drove straight to my son's Little League coach, told him what happened and gave him all the baseballs.

Everybody was happy.

25

Real Man

Carol had a down cow, well she was almost down. She had calved a couple days earlier and had a condition we call Grass Tetany. It's a sudden loss of magnesium in the blood. This causes a loss of coordination. It's most common in spring and winter months, and around the time when they have their calves. Sometimes they die so quickly all you find is a dead cow. Others are down and can't get up. Some others, like this cow could get up. That wouldn't as such be a problem, but these cows are belligerent, aggressive and think killing you is just fine.

That was this cow.

She was down in an open field with no trees or any protection around. I couldn't drive my truck there either. It was spring, and the pastures were soggy. This was going to be a little tricky, or maybe worse.

As we got to her, she stood to charge but was wobbly and fell back down. I roped her with my lariat. She got back up. I pulled her to one side, and she went back down. Quickly, actually really quickly, I made the lariat into a halter and tied it to her back leg. She was secure, and better yet, we were safe. I started the IV treatment.

There was going to be a problem, however. My treatment would make her better. She would be better coordinated, but still nasty. This goes away later. Maybe much later.

I explained this to Carol. We both looked around for escape routes. The closest were some willow bushes a good sprint away. At least Carol could get away. I would try to fend for myself which I had done before.

Near the end of my IV treatment, Bobby showed up across the field. He was a Carol's friend. I was never sure what he did for a living. Sometimes he was a substitute sheriff for little towns around Oregon. He did carry a gun, and it was always strapped to his hip in a holster. I was immediately relieved. I figured I had a real man to help.

He made his way to us while I was still treating the cow. I explained the situation to Bobby: the cow danger, the need to get Carol away and that I needed help releasing the cow. Two would always be better than one. Two could distract and confuse the cow and maybe make it safer.

Finally, I finished the IV, pulled the needle, told Carol to get going and hide in the bushes. She was gone in a flash. I was quick about it, untying the cow, and taking the lariat off. I looked around for Bobby to help. No Bobby. He ran to the bushes with Carol.

The cow stood up, saw me and started towards me. I dodged her and she fell back. I ran the direction she wasn't looking and finally circled back to my truck. We all made it safely.

As I drove away, I realized you can't judge a man by the gun he's wearing.

26

About My Rope

MY ROPE IS REALLY a lariat used for lassoing animals. I call it my rope because, well, that's a common term out here for your lariat.

Today, most are made out of nylon or a similar synthetic material. Hemp lariats were common in the past. They're not as strong and rain or moisture really affects them. Today's lariats are really strong in all weather, you can pull your truck with one.

Mine belonged to a rodeo cowboy who used it so much it lost its stiffness and doesn't hold a good loop anymore. Not for a rodeo cowboy anyway. For me it's fine. I want a softer rope for my hands and tying knots.

I'm not much of a roper. In fact, I have very limited talent at roping. OK, let's face it, I'm lousy at roping. I think I'm just good enough to usually get the job done, but not good enough for people to truly rely on me.

My roping is usually done on the ground rather on a horse, so it's all a bit different.

Sometimes, I've tried to rope from a fence or even tree limb. Mixed results. Once I roped a very aggressive, if not outright dangerous, cow from the roof of my pickup. She had a blood mineral deficiency, Grass Tetany, that caused her nasty and dangerous behavior. I caught her, she ran into the side of my pickup, turned and ran away with my rope. I hadn't thought that out very well. I should have stayed in my pickup. It wouldn't be dented, and I'd still have my rope. I went home empty handed, literally.

I try to rope animals in an enclosed space, like a pen, stall, or small corral. That's so I can get close enough and they don't have too far to run after I catch them, if I catch them. Also, I try not to get the animals excited and will toss my rope underhand. It's a little sneakier and less disturbing to the animal.

Once they are caught, I look for something to wrap the rope around. A fencepost is good, so is a tree, or maybe a bumper on someone else's truck, not mine. Trailer hitches work well too.

Two wraps around a post will hold most things. In fact, there's an old adage that says two wraps enable a boy to hold a bull. Maybe the rope won't slip, but a bull could most likely pull the fencepost out of the ground, maybe even pull out a little tree.

What do I try to rope? Usually calves, sheep, goats, llamas and sometimes a young horse. Not pigs, however, they are lousy candidates because they are fast, smart, excellent in 4-wheel drive and often can run right through a lariat loop. Sheep and llamas are hard because they're quick with their necks. I have my best luck with them when it's almost dark and they can't see my rope very well. Although that's usually when I'd rather be home after working all day.

I'm not a fan of roping full sized cows and especially bulls. Too big and strong. But, I do it anyway. They're usually too sick or lame to do much. If they're really sick, the rope around the neck can choke them too much and that could create more problems, like killing the animal you want to treat.

Calves are easier just because they're smaller and not as strong. However, they can be a handful regardless.

As I've gotten older, I've purposefully lowered my roping competency. In fact, at this point I'm downright stupid with a lariat. It took me a long time to figure out I didn't need to be a cowboy. It's better for my body too.

27

A I in the Country

LET'S get this straight to start with. We're not talking about Artificial Intelligence. This is a reproductive subject. Artificial Insemination.

It's been common in livestock for years, especially in cattle and pigs. Less so in horses, and even less than that in the other farm animals.

But here we're talking about humans.

Kendra brought an older new horse by to be looked over. Teeth work, vaccinations, deworming, and a concerning, old leg scar. It was for her niece. He was fine for his age, gentle too.

I had known Kendra for a long time and soon we got to talking.

"How are things in the mountains?" I asked.

She lived on a small farm in the mountains, had a job,

took care of her mother, and had a small herd of cattle. She was now in her late thirties. No men that I knew, but then things can change quickly.

She told me about her cattle. Up to 30 head now. A bull, 10 cows, 10 new calves and 10 older calves. She raised the calves until two years old, then sold them to customers already butchered, cut and wrapped, and ready to eat. Nice little side business.

Her mom was doing fine too considering her health issues.

"Next time you see me, I might be pregnant," she casually said.

"What are you talking about?"I asked a bit incredulously.

"Well, I'm in my late thirties so I don't have much time left."

"Uh, do you have a partner?" I wasn't sure how to ask this question.

"Nope, I'm going to do it AI."

"But you still need a donor." I replied.

"My best friend's brother will do it."

"Do you know him?" again incredulously, I asked.

"Yep. He got hurt some years back and is in a wheelchair. He's a nice guy. He'll even help support the kid."

People wheelchair bound aren't always functional at everything I was thinking. "Can he, like, do it?" I asked.

"He says he can. Sometimes anyway."

"Where are you doing it?"

She looked at me like I was crazy and for some reason did not understand human parts. "I mean the clinic, hospital, or whatever,"to clarify my question.

"I talked to Kaiser, my insurance company, but they said they would only do it if the natural way failed."

"So, what's next?" This was getting interesting.

"Well, I figure we have two possibilities. He's able to do it, we put it in a turkey baster, and you know the rest. Or, we have some drinks, get pretty drunk, and get into to bed together and see what happens."

"Good luck and let me know how it goes." I replied. I'm still incredulous, but even more so how casual and matter of fact Kendra was about all this.

"That's the no nonsense approach of a woman who raises cattle," I thought.

She said she would for sure keep me updated.

28

A rchie and My Lariat

ARCHIE WAS OLD, really old. He drove around in beat up, little, faded red pickup truck. He had large thick glasses and drove down the middle of road. His dog sat beside him looking out the front window just like a passenger. It you saw him coming, you got out of the way.

At this point, he was near the end of his empire and most likely his life. He had an assortment of small ranches where he ran cattle. Things were pretty much broken down, sort of like him.

One day he called and told me he had a cow and her sick calf in a wood corral south of town. I knew the place, not much of a corral, however. I took my assistant Dan because I didn't think I could do this alone.

That afternoon we arrived and found them. The cow

was what was politely called snorty. That means she could get nasty or explode on us. Quickly, too.

I looked over the situation and decided I needed to lasso the calf, so I could look it over and give medication. I suspected it had pneumonia. We both got in the corral. I had my lariat and told Dan to move the pair past me. That was easy since the cow didn't want to be around us. That was much better than charging us, however.

I stood at the halfway point in the corral. Dan moved the cow past me. The calf was slower because it was sick. My goal was lassoing the calf and as the cow stopped at the end of the corral, I would wrap my lariat around some part of the corral.

I did manage to lasso the calf, which was not a given with my limited talents. Just as I was ready wrap the rope around a post, the cow, with now a head of steam, ran right through the end of the corral. She broke all the boards! The calf was right behind her and moved so fast it tore the lariat from hands.

The last thing I saw of them was the cow running as fast as possible to the river with the calf and lariat behind her.

I was pretty upset, if not just indignant. Maybe I wasn't really much of a roper, but I needed my lariat because they were fairly expensive in those days. I drove to his house knowing he wasn't home but hoping his wife was. She was. I explained what happened and how expensive my lariat was. I exaggerated the value a bit hoping to speed things up. I knew he wouldn't like to buy me a new lariat. He was pretty cheap. Actually, he was really cheap. She seemed concerned and said she would tell Archie.

About 6:30 the next morning I heard a knocking on the door. There was Archie and lariat. I was more than surprised and thanked him profusely.

I never figured out how this old man, fairly crippled at that and with bad eyes, managed to get a hold of the calf and remove my lariat.

However, I'm pretty sure the motivation was simply about money.

29

Blackberries, Old Cars, a Crooked House

LIZ WAS GOOD WITH HORSES. Really good. She could train or retrain almost any horse. In fact, she turned this talent into a business and actually made money. That's pretty much unheard of in the horse world.

"Wait," you're saying, "What does this have to do with blackberries, old cars and a crooked house?"

Stick with me and we'll get there.

Liz visited livestock auctions and sought out the horses. Usually, the horses were divided into two group. One group was the good horses that were expected to sell for riding, or work, or show, or breeding. The other was the kill pen. They were going to go for slaughter. Most of these were old, broken down, usually really broken down, or untrainable outlaws. But there were others too, the unlucky ones. They might be just fine, but unlucky. Maybe the owner died, went bankrupt, got divorced, imprisoned, or experienced some other unspeakable human tragedy.

These were the ones Liz was looking for and she had a good eye.

This means she could pick a good prospect by just spending time watching the horse.

She would buy these horses at a discount because they weren't considered important or valuable.

Liz would then bring them by our clinic for a health checkup which could include routine things like vaccinations, deworming, teeth work, maybe x-rays or even seeing if a mare with a big belly was pregnant.

Then she would take them home for retraining or a tune up as it is often called. After that, she would advertise them online. She had a good reputation and sold the horses easily. People trusted her, and they should.

Almost always, she brought Jake, her partner, along to our clinic. I'm not really sure of their relationship, but he was always supportive and easy to get along with. I'm not sure what he did job wise, maybe worked at a mill. That would make sense since this is timber country.

They had a side business too. They fixed up old houses, maybe barns also. There is always a need for people willing to fix up old houses and other buildings.

One day, while working on a new horse she claimed from an auction, she and Jake started telling me about their latest construction project.

Someone had a house they wanted to sell. It needed help. The house sat at the bottom of a steep hill which was slowly sliding into the house. The house was no longer level. It was completely surrounded by blackberry vines which had essentially gone rogue.

Liz and Jake looked through the house. It was definitely

crooked. A marble or baseball would roll from the hillside of the house to the other end of it. Easily.

Jake decided to look under the house to see if had a foundation, or just what was under it.

As he was looking around under the house, Liz looked around the yard full of blackberry vines.

They quickly discovered two things:

One, the house was jacked up with car jacks. It had no foundation, just car jacks on pieces of wood.

Two, the blackberries were full of old, abandoned cars.

Jake found his machete and chopped his way to some of the cars. Each one had an open trunk with a missing jack!

Apparently, it was cheaper and easier to buy junker cars and use their jacks to keep the house somewhat level than putting a foundation under it.

30

B onding

OVER MANY, many years of working with men and women in difficult and dangerous situations, special friendships develop. I call this bonding.

It was night, of course, a winter night, of course, filled with heavy winds and rain, of course. Almost cold enough to snow but not, of course.

The heifer had calved in all this. She had worked hard to expel a too large and now dead calf. If that wasn't bad enough, her uterus followed the calf out.

That's how Tom found her while making his last checks on that terrible winter evening. Fortunately, she was strong enough to be herded to a nearby corral.

That's when Tom called me.

The weather was relentless. The mud was deep, the kind that pulls your boots off.

We suited up, rain boots, rain pants, rain jackets and some sort of a hat that wouldn't blow away.

The heifer was subdued by all this. I was able to walk right up to her, put my rope around her neck, make it into a halter so she wouldn't choke.

Then we started to work.

It wasn't hard to clean the uterus. The rain washed it clean, and the wind blew the water off.

That was the easy part.

Then Tom held up the uterus for me and I began the unbelievable job of replacing it. Putting it back in the heifer. As quiet and exhausted as she was, she managed to push it back out twice.

It kept raining. The wind kept blowing. And it kept getting colder.

Finally, I got it in, all the way. It stayed too.

I gave her drugs for infection, pain, shock and to keep it in place.

She survived. So did we, but it was a miserable time for all of us.

Tom and I never forgot that evening together.

Many years later he told me that she not only lived, but thrived. She gave birth another 10-12 times. All successful.

31

Calling the Cops on Yourself

IT WAS Saturday and Joe had worked a hard week. He was a farrier and one of the best. He trimmed and shod horses. That's hard, very hard work. After all, horses weigh 1000 pounds or more and are not always cooperative.

Joe's friend, Fred, was over and they were trying to get Joe's 1950 Ford pickup running. Fred was the real mechanic of the two. Joe mostly held his new iPhone, using it as a flashlight so Fred could see.

They were also drinking beer, actually quite a bit of beer.

Later, much later, in the day after rebuilding the starter and charging the battery, they started up the truck. It sounded fine.

"Let's take it for run," Fred suggested.

Joe was wary. They had been drinking a lot, and he did

not want to get stopped for drinking and driving. He had to drive to make a living.

'I don't know," he replied.

"Look Joe, we're way out the country. There's no traffic, or anybody around. We can go down to that wide spot and turn around, where the old store and gas station used to be."

"OK, we can do that," Joe relented.

The old truck ran great. Soon they got to the turn around.

Suddenly, Joe thought, "Where is my phone?"

"Fred, I don't know where my phone is."

"Maybe you set it on the fender or somewhere under the hood. That means it probably fell out onto the road," Fred speculated.

They started back but soon found a Sheriff's patrol car in their lane. It was driving very slowly, like maybe they were looking for something.

Following the patrol car would take forever, but Joe didn't want to draw any attention either. Finally, he passed the patrol at a reasonable speed, he hoped.

Just before he got home an ambulance approached from the other direction. It quickly passed them. "What is going on?" Joe and Fred wondered.

They got back to Joe's place. He told his wife about the phone, but didn't mention the patrol car and ambulance. It was dark now. She suggested each take a flashlight, look down the driveway and then start down the road.

They were no sooner on the road when a firetruck came by and stopped. The driver got out and curtly asked, "What are you doing?"

Joe was taken aback by his attitude but answered, "Looking for my cell phone. It fell out of my truck."

"So are we," the firetruck driver replied.

Then he explained what happened.

When the cell phone hit the road and was seriously damaged it sent out an emergency warning. This was a new safety feature. The phone assumed the damage meant there was a car wreck and immediately sent a warning and the location as well.

"Oh, my god!" Joe thought. "I was so careful to drive where nobody would be around especially after drinking so much beer. So what I ended up doing was calling the cops on myself."

32

Canoes as Hitching Posts

DONNA WAS FRANTIC. "Doc, you've got to come take care of my horse. He got hurt."

I had two problems:

One, I had just returned home, it was evening, and I had had a long day. However, that was my life.

Two was the real problem. Her horse didn't like me. He got very, very nervous when I showed up. I really couldn't handle him, and usually injured horses take some serious care which requires some serious handling.

"Ok, I'll head over. It will take me about 45 minutes, maybe an hour."

It was dark when I arrived. The horse was in a small barn. I needed my flashlight to see him. He was both excited and nervous, but I was able to look him over from a distance. He could move normally, had some abrasions and one leg was slightly swollen. However, no cuts that needed stitches. That sort of surprised me since I knew she only had barbed wire fences.

"I think he'll be fine. I can leave you some drugs to help with the swelling. You can mix it in his grain. I'm surprised he's not cut up from your fences."

She was quiet.

"Tell him what happened," her husband said.

She told me she had gone to the pasture to bring the horse in for the night. Unfortunately, she found the gate hard to open while holding the horse. She needed to tie him up until she got the gate open.

Looking around, she found an 18-foot aluminum canoe.

That was an "aha" moment and so she tied her horse to the canoe.

Something happened, maybe the gate made weird noise, or maybe its movement did. The horse spooked, turned and ran. Right after him came the canoe. Aluminum canoes are noisy, really noisy. The faster the horse, the faster the canoe chased it. Sometimes it hit the horse's hind legs. I'm sure the horse thought it was going to die. Finally, the rope broke and horse was free.

Lesson to be learned: don't tie your horse to a canoe, especially an aluminum canoe.

33

Charley's Very, Very Special Weekend

CHARLEY WAS A GOAT, a big brown and white neutered male. He had long floppy ears. Actually, he was quite handsome.

He came to me in the back of a sheriff's car on a cold, wet wintry day. The Deputy had found him loose and being attacked by a couple dogs. There was no owner to be found, or at least one who would claim him.

His injuries turned out to be rather minor. I agreed to keep him at my barn in the meantime.

Soon he was well, however I was unable to find the owner. I did learn that he was an escape artist. Maybe the last owner decided Charley, the name we gave him, was now on his own after too many escapes.

He adjusted well, but I suspect now he was used to adjusting to new situations. I put him with my small sheep flock. As it turned out, he really didn't care about befriending sheep and soon escaped. I patched fences and he still escaped. This went on for quite a while until it seemed I had found all the holes in my fences, even things I didn't think were holes.

As I said before, he was quite handsome and as it turned out had a captivating personality. Now that I had found and patched all the escape holes, we really enjoyed having him around.

It was summer and we were retuning from visiting relatives in the southern end of the state. Our older neighbor, Margaret, had assigned herself to watch over our place. She was very serious and thorough about her responsibility.

Suddenly, during our quiet and relaxed drive home, she called on her cell phone. She was hysterical. Charley had disappeared. She had searched and searched without finding him. Actually, I wasn't overly concerned because his escapes had become exhausting. I told her not to worry that I would search for him when we got home.

Margaret was not the type to forget about him and go home. Anyway, she really had nothing else to do.

It wasn't long before she called back. She had found Charley. He was in the house on the couch looking out the window. Now she was really hysterical, and I was, for the moment, more worried about her. I thought maybe she would have a heart attack, or stroke because she was so excited.

After some talking, she and I decided to have her contact two neighbor women to help.

The doors were locked, but there was a dog door for big dogs, and apparently a certain goat. One of the neighbors crawled far enough through the dog door to open the regular door. They quickly caught Charley, after all he was quite friendly, and locked him safely in the barn.

Then they assessed the house. It was a mess. He had peed and pooped everywhere for several hours, on the rug, on the beds, on the couch.

Our wonderful neighbors cleaned up the worst and I am eternally thankful for their help. Still, it took months to clean up after Charley.

Let's face it, when it's all said and done, Charley had a very, very special weekend.

34

Curt

CURT WAS from a small town to the east. He had pretty much spent his whole life there. He wasn't a big man, but he was strong and wiry. He was fearless too.

For many years he worked at the mill but could almost do anything. He could fix houses, reroof, rewire, replumb, or just build the whole thing. He could also fix cars, pickups and tractors.

He had horses and mules that he raised and trained. Along the way, he had learned to shoe horses and mules. He became a pretty reliable cowboy farrier, more than just a good farrier. Curt could shoe anything regardless of the difficulty and danger, particularly the danger. He had a long, thick cotton rope he used to tie up and restrain the bad ones. He worked on all the horses and mules nobody else could or would do.

Although I had trained and experienced help, I liked to use Curt in some situations, like mainly handling and doing vet work on nasty and dangerous horses and mules. Truthfully, I didn't want my help to get hurt. I was willing to take my own chances, but not the help's chances.

Curt was only too willing to help. He was good and reliable, maybe a little crazy too. Maybe we both were.

Glenn had a couple of 10-year-old stallions. He didn't do anything with them and they just ran in the fields with his cattle. He wasn't a cattleman either as he raised mink. The cattle kept the grass down. I'm not sure why he had the horses. Maybe it was an old girlfriend's idea.

They weren't really wild like just off the range. They just were not trained or ever, ever handled.

Finally, he decided they needed to be gelded because he just didn't need two mature stallions running about his place. Maybe it was because of new grandkids that were now running about. That was certainly a good, very good reason. Roaming stallions aren't always predictable and safe.

Glenn called one day to set up an appointment. The horses needed their feet trimmed too. It had been years, I suspected.

I asked about catching the two stallions. He couldn't catch them, but he could get them in a small corral with a cattle chute. Cattle handling equipment is not safe for horses as too many things can go wrong. There are too many ways horses can get hurt, especially on the metal.

In spite of more than serious misgivings, I agreed. I also asked Curt to help. Naturally, he was more than willing. To him it sounded like the most fun he'd had in years. To me it sounded like a great disaster lurking.

On the given day and time, Curt and I arrived to find

Glenn waiting for us. As promised, he had the two stallions caught. They were quietly eating some lousy hay that was probably several years old and really for cattle.

He quickly told me he had to leave. He had a haircut appointment!

Truthfully, I thought he probably didn't want to be anywhere around when we worked on the horses. I really didn't blame him, but was a bit disappointed if for nothing more than having someone to call 911 in an emergency.

Curt and I looked over the situation. We figured the wood corral would hold the horses as long they didn't get too excited. Then we looked over the cattle chute and put tape over all the sharp edges and points.

We were ready to go.

To my astonishment, Curt got in the coral and worked one the horses into the cattle chute. I closed both ends. He climbed out and put a halter on the horse. At that point we had everything set and ready to go with my surgery equipment and his foot trimming tools.

I gave the horse two IV injections. As it started to wobble from the drugs, we opened the front of the chute and it stumbled out. That was better than we expected. We dragged it off to the side. I did my surgery, and he was now a gelding. It was now Curt's turn. Quickly and expertly, he trimmed the feet that were several years past due.

We wanted to get the second before the first one woke up and did who knows what.

Curt got back in the corral and got the second stallion in the cattle chute. I closed both ends again. We repeated the process. Now we had two geldings with freshly trimmed feet.

We stayed around long enough to see them recover from

the drugs, get up, and start nibbling on grass along the edges.

They were in Glenns' hands now, whenever he got back from his haircut.

More important - nobody got hurt, horses or people.

35

Full Body Prayer

BRANDON and his family had moved north from Los Angeles. It was time to get out of the madness infecting their lives.

They were neighbors. Just down the road or over the little creek and through some woods depending on how you went. He bought a couple horses that I would occasionally care for.

He seemed to stay occupied at different jobs but also started a church. A small church.

After 40 years I had worn out my left hip. I'm left-handed, so, I think I probably led with my left leg holding some animal I had roped. I was reluctant to blame other things I did like carry heavy loads backpacking, or mountain climbing, running, or playing basketball.

Anyway, it got to be time for a new hip. I was ready, too. I was tired of the pain and inability to things I really enjoyed.

Near my surgery date, I was at Brandon's looking at a horse problem. I mentioned my upcoming surgery. He was very concerned and sympathetic. That's the way he was.

"When you get really close to your surgery, call me and I'll come over and give you a prayer."

Although praying had fallen to the wayside in my life, I was genuinely moved by his offer. "I will," I answered.

Finally, the time came near and I called him. He came over later one afternoon after work for both of us.

We went into the kitchen, and he started his prayer for me. He began at my head, praying, touching. He spent a lot of time at my bad hip. He finished at my feet.

I was raised in a reserved church, quiet prayers and certainly no touching. His prayer was full of emotion, energy, and concern. I was really impressed by the effort he put into my prayer.

Finally, he finished, stood up, gave me a pat on the back and said, "You're good to go."

He was right, I healed quickly and was back to caring for horses and cattle in 3-4 weeks.

Thanks Brandon.

36

George's New Fence

THERE IS a small lane that runs through our place and past the barn I used as a vet office and clinic. George and Margaret lived at the end of the lane. It was an old homestead that Margaret's family had owned since the late 1800's.

At this point in their lives, Margaret worked in a fish processing plant and George was a pile buck. That's somebody who drives pilings. In this case, mainly in the Columbia River. He didn't work all that much anymore, but he did drink his whiskey regularly.

ONE EVENING after working on farms around our area, I was taking down a fence to put in new posts and then putting it back up. We had a small flock of sheep, but they were in another pasture at the moment.

. . .

MY YOUNG SON was helping me. Matt was about ten then. We had laid the fence on out along the lane. The far end of it curled up off the ground.

AS WE WERE PUTTING new posts in, George came by on his way home. Friendly and fuzzy, as usual. We talked for a while, probably heard another war story. Another one we had already heard. Finally, he headed down the lane to home.

I WASN'T PAYING much attention as he left as I wanted to get the fence back up before dark.

SUDDENLY, my son started yelling and pointing to the truck driving away.

George's truck bumper had hooked the curled-up end of the fence. He drove off completely unaware of what was happening.

IN FACT, he drove all the way home with the fence. About a quarter of a mile trailing fifty feet of fence. Then he parked the truck, got out and walked to their house. He didn't have a clue as to what had just happened.

FINALLY, I stopped laughing. That took a while too.

. . .

I THOUGHT I could have a little fun with this ridiculous situation so I called Margaret.

"MARGARET, I'm missing a fence. Could you take a look behind George's pickup?"

OF COURSE, she thought I was nuts, but she did go look and sure enough discovered my missing fence.

I DIDN'T ASK George to bring it back. My son and I went down, rolled it up and brought it home. Anyway, George was probably busy getting a bit fuzzier after a haranguing from Margaret.

How Not to Pay a Bill

EVERYBODY WHO RUNS A SMALL BUSINESS, and that's what a country vet does, needs to get paid. Most of us run on a narrow margin in our finances which is probably our own fault. We probably don't charge enough, and no doubt give credit unwisely. Plus, we feel sorry for the animals. We send people bills and wait for the money. However, the quicker it comes in, the better our lives are.

As it turns out, there seem to be a few people who specialize in not paying their bills. It's not like they are mistreating you in particular, it's how they operate. They treat everybody that way.

Let's say Willard Taylor seems unusually good at not paying his vet bills and I wonder about him. So, then I ask a friend, a friend who has a small business.

"Do you know Willard Taylor?" I ask.

"Yeah, he doesn't pay his bills. Get cash only," he replies immediately, even before I can tell him my problem.

Anyway, I learned it's not personal, except when I can't pay my bills.

These people are pretty clever about how they do it.

Don't put a stamp on the envelope. Great technique for delaying payment until they can shift some funds around. By the time the envelope gets back to Willard, and then back to me with a stamp it's been weeks.

Wrong address, incorrect address or illegible address, these are like having no stamp. It takes weeks to cycle back to where you get it. Hopefully.

Don't sign the check. This wasn't a problem years ago when banks were local and small. They would take the check anyway, or you could forge it if they knew you.

Wrong numbers? There are lots of possibilities here.

The date on the check can be way off in the future. Then you can't cash the check for weeks, or months or whenever.

Or the numbers can be totally wrong, usually not enough, but maybe just conflicting. Anyway, it just messes up the check and you can't use it because the bank won't accept it.

On very rare occasions, the check is written for too much. Definitely shocking.

I always call the person and explain it. If it's just a little more, they may say just apply to future bills, but if it's really big I tear up the check.

These days, it's all different. Everybody has a credit card, and everybody has a cell phone. Easy to pay right on the spot with no regrets later.

38

Before the War

EDWIN LIVED down one of the river valleys and had a small dairy. He milked six Guernsey cows. That's actually a very small dairy. If you don't know, Guernseys are large brown and white cows with very placid, if not sweet, dispositions. They give the most delightfully rich milk. Probably unhealthy, but delicious.

He was raised on this little farm by a couple that adopted him as a child. Edwin never left the place. By the time I got to know him, he was older, near retirement or more. He seemed like somebody who was always older. Tall at one time, now stooped with wispy, graying hair. He spoke softly. It took a while to get to know him. His wife, at one time, worked in the fish plants in town. She was retired now and had difficulty getting around. I wasn't sure how they made enough money to live on. Milking six cows?

With just six cows and their offspring, he didn't really need me much. Although over several years I made enough visits to get to know him. Anyway, there's always lots of time to talk while doing vet work on cows. I think he was lonely too. He lived an isolated life.

Somehow, he discovered George was my neighbor. It turns out they grew up near each other in this same river valley. It became routine for Edwin to ask about George. And because he was my neighbor, I could always give him an update.

These questions about George and my answers had gone on for several years by now and it seemed to me they must be pretty good friends by maybe staying in contact someway.

Finally, one day I asked Edwin, "When was the last time you saw George?"

Edwin stared out the barn window thinking. After some time, he turned and said, "Just before the war."

He was talking about WorldWar II.

39

Kelsey's Unexpected Birthday Gift

KELSEY IS MY GRANDDAUGHTER. She has red hair and the rest of her goes along with that, if you know what I mean. Particularly her sense of humor which is large and trends to the weird. I happen to think a sense of humor, one trending toward weird, is an essential survival skill in this world. Today, tomorrow, anywhere, anytime.

Anyway, it's her birthday and we're supposed to show up at her party, a party of eight year olds and some brave and dedicated parents.

Her parents live just out of town on hill where there are a few other houses around, but it's pretty rural. That's where the party is.

At the last moment, I get a phone call. The people are distraught, maybe even worse. They just got home from work to find their young horse down, probably dead. It's maybe two to three months old. Too young to die. I send my wife ahead without me so I can attend to this disaster before the party.

I drive straight there, about 40 minutes away. The animal is dead and has been for a while, most of the day and long enough for rigor mortis to set in. I can't tell much from the surface. The poor folks are extremely upset. They left a healthy young horse in the morning and came home to it mysteriously dead. It's heart breaking for the animal and the people.

I will need to cut it open, do a necropsy to discover what happened, what went wrong. I don't want to do it in front of them as they're already too upset. Anyway, I have a birthday party to go to.

"Look," I say, "I can probably find out what happened, but I have more things to do yet." Of course, I didn't say that meant going to my granddaughter's birthday party. "I'll take him with me and look him over at home later. I can bury him for you too. I'll get back to you later about my findings."

My pickup has a canopy which works well in our rainy world. I built a plywood box of drawers and spaces for all my drugs, vaccines, syringes, needles, surgical gear and all sort other things you can't even imagine.

There is gap between the box and tailgate, maybe 15 inches or so. That's where I need to put the dead horse. Of course, with rigor mortis he doesn't fold up. We get him in upside down with his legs sticking out. Rather unsightly at best. Anyway, I head to the party late, of course.

I arrive mid party. The party is in the front yard, because there's some construction work in back. My granddaughter recognizes my truck and runs up as I drive up. She immediately sees the young dead horse's feet protruding. "Papa, what did you bring?"

A few girls run up with her, and an especially adroit one opens the tailgate, and the horse tips onto the tailgate. Kelsey and her two brave and curious friends were completely enthralled. Most of the other kids flee, as do their mothers. They are aghast. I'm not sure but a couple may simply have left in their cars at that point.

After that, I was given explicit instruction about what I could and could not bring to birthday parties for my grandkids.

However, even today, many years later, Kelsey thinks that was just a wonderful present.

40

The Last Time

HIS HORSE WAS DOWN and dying. It wasn't too surprising since it was very old and not doing well. The horse had lost a lot of weight during the winter and was now very skinny. It was time to put it down.

Phil lived to the south some distance and it took a while to get there. The cold, early spring rain let up by the time I arrived. The old horse was laying just outside the barn under a tree.

He had had horses for years and used them mainly for hunting in the high mountain in eastern part of the state. He was very fond of them. They were old horses now and not used much.

I only saw the down horse, although I was sure he had another one.

I didn't spend much time examining it, nor trying to

convince Phil we could try for a miracle. It was time to be merciful, not heroic.

As I prepared my drugs and we walked back to the horse he said, "I hope this goes better than last time."

Well, that confused me since I could not remember putting down a horse for him. I asked, "What are you taking about?"

Then he explained. He had found his other old horse down last fall. He figured since he was a hunter, he could dispatch it with his rifle. Actually, shooting a horse in the correct area of the head can be very successful as well as merciful. But if you miss, well that's a disaster.

He shot the horse in the head but missed the vital area. The horse got up immediately and ran away from him. Phil was horrified by his failure and followed the horse to finish things. But the horse, although dying, was frightened and would not let him get near it for another shot.

Finally, after much time and careful stalking, he was able to get into a position for another shot and bring the horse down for good.

It was horrible for the horse and for him. The horse had been a longtime companion, and he felt terrible about it.

I administered my drugs to the down horse and it died peacefully as it deserved.

41

Mikko

HE HAD the cow caught for me. Well, sort of. She was in a makeshift pen, part barn wall, part old bulldozer and some rickety livestock panels. The cow wasn't very happy, but her foot hurt too much for her to do anything. Her left front hoof was swollen and infected. She needed some antibiotics, an injection that would last several days.

"Use your lasso and I'll help you," Mikko said.

He was a big bear like man, and I was sure he could help. I got my lariat and roped her. That was pretty easy, she couldn't move much.

Once I tightened the lariat around her neck, things changed. She exploded, pain or no pain. She ran through one end of the corral and was gone out into the field. My lariat was ripped from my hands and was with her in the field. She didn't go far though as it hurt too much.

I looked at Mikko. He said, "I'll get my tractor."

Shortly, he was back with his 1950 vintage gray Ford tractor. They run forever, maybe not well, but forever. "Bring what you need," he said, and motioned me to join him on the tractor. I sat on one of the big back fenders. I had no idea what he had in mind.

We chugged our way to the cow. She moved away. Mikko kept at it. The cow kept moving away, but less each time she moved. Finally, she just stood still. Mikko then drove the tractor tire on my lariat. She was caught just feet away.

I used another rope I had brought along to make a halter and gave it to Mikko. He held it and I injected the drugs. It was done just like that. I was amazed.

On the way back he asked, "Do you want a beer?"

It was a warm afternoon, and we had sort of performed a miracle, so I said, "Sure."

He drove us to the house just up the hill, got off his tractor and walked over his pickup, an old Ford too. He dropped the tailgate and said, "We can sit here." The tailgate had a big dent in it, like a lot of farm trucks. He went to the house and shortly returned with a six pack of cheap beer. That was fine. Cheap beer and a warm day seem to go together.

Mikko drank two beers while I took two sips. He threw the cans over his shoulder into the pickup bed behind us. He was a quiet man, always. He spoke with an accent from his Finnish upbringing. He was a brooding man too and I wasn't sure what that was all about.

Then he began to talk, to tell me his story.

He was born in eastern Finland along the Russian border. They had land, lots of land and it had been in the family for generations.

The land included a large valley with a river running

through it, pastureland, cattle, horses, crop land, fish in the river, timber in the hills along the sides. It was enough for all of them, he and his two brothers, forever.

Then the war came. The big war and the Bear came. It moved the border and took their land. Took everything. They fled west, eventually making it to America.

Now Mikko worked at the mill and ran a few cows on his small farm.

He never forgot what was taken from them. The loss cast a deep, black shadow over him. He was forever changed.

I listened and hardly said a word. This man who rarely talked had just told me his long and tragic story.

The afternoon waned and began to cool.

I left and drove home, forever changed by his story.

42

Mountain Lions

SOME YEARS ago there was a Mountain Lion fad. People, for some reason, had to have these big cats as pets. The animals were usually defanged and declawed to lessen their danger to the owners and others.

Fortunately, this fad was short lived.

There was a man in a nearby town who had one. He drove around proudly showing his lion to everybody. He had a a 1970 model Lincoln convertible. He kept the top down, and the lion collared and chained in the back.

He loved to park in front of Safeway while his wife was shopping.

That way everybody could see his animal. He probably also needed to make sure that some totally stupid person would not try to pet it.

It always appeared calm, demur and spectacularly beautiful but scary as hell too.

Eventually he lost interest, and the big cat was no longer seen. I'm not sure what happened to it, or him either, as far as that goes.

Keith had a couple horses that need some routine spring care. I was there for a look over and give vaccinations.

He also had a Mountain Lion. His was kept well secured behind cyclone fencing. The pen was about 40 feet long, maybe 20 feet wide and 15 feet high. In one end was a loft where the big cat could sleep, rest, or whatever.

Keith was holding both horses in front of the pen with the lion inside. They seemed completely unconcerned about the big cat's presence.

As I started my care of the horses a small bird got through the fencing. Maybe a Starling. It was at the far end from the Mountain Lion.

The fluttering of the bird awoke the dozing lion. Instantaneously, the big cat was down from its loft, crossed the length of the pen, and leaped up to the bird in the upper corner. It captured the bird in its paw.

I'm not sure I really saw its movement from one end of the pen to the other. It was that fast. It was startlingly fast. I always knew these cats were amazing and ferocious hunters, but I had never witnessed one in action.

This was humbling. It was scary. But most of all, it garnered my utmost respect. Mountain Lions possess physical abilities we can barely imagine. In this case, I could barely see what happened.

43

O striches

THERE WAS A TIME, not that many years ago, that ostriches became quite popular. They were touted as an investment. Naturally, it was just another pyramid scheme. Fortunately, it died a quick death.

If you don't know, these are big, big birds. They can stand seven to eight feet tall and weigh over 200 pounds. They have lousy personalities and would just as soon attack you as anything. Their weapons are their enormous beaks that can break skulls or their large sharp toes that can eviscerate you.

As I said, the fad was short lived mainly because they weren't any fun and in fact, very dangerous. Also, they didn't reproduce well so there were not enough new birds to sell. New birds were where the profit was. Typical for a pyramid scheme.

Regardless, they did show up in my area and several clients had them.

Once, I had horse under anesthesia and I was ready to do surgery. Suddenly, 6 ostriches appeared along the fence behind me. They were so tall that they could reach over the fence and touch me. I made the owner drive them away and keep them away so I could finish the surgery. Pretty unnerving.

I realized quickly that I needed a policy for dealing with ostriches. Actually, I didn't want to deal with them at all.

Finally, I decided my new policy was that I would not handle and care for birds bigger than me.

44

Problems with Horseshoes

FRANK WAS A PRETTY good cowboy farrier. I'm not sure where he learned his trade, but he could do all the basic things on horses, mules and donkeys, good or bad. He could nail on a basic set of shoes, and they would stay on.

He was good with animals and the people. Everybody liked him.

One summer he took on shoeing horses for a dude string. These horses were rented out for people to ride and almost always with a guide to keep things safe. If nothing else, dude horses have to be quiet and safe in all situations.

Most of the horses are older. Maybe up to forty years old. But they are quiet and safe. Some of them need drugs to help with arthritis and some need special shoeing. The special shoeing was where Frank came in.

Because of some long-term changes in the older horses'

feet, an abnormality developed that required some help. These horses had a condition called founder. It's complex, but eventually the hoof on the outside misaligns with the bone inside. That causes the center of gravity of the foot systems to change.

There are a lot of fancy things you can do for this situation, but they take time and money. That rarely works in dude horse situations.

There was an old technique any farrier could use to help this situation. Even a cowboy farrier could put the shoes on backwards so the rounded end extended out past the back of the hoof. This wasn't a cure, but it changed the center of gravity and made the horse more comfortable and useful.

I had already selected the old horses that needed this kind of shoeing.

I showed Frank what to do and he carried this on for the summer riding season.

Later that fall, I ran into Frank shoeing horses. I was curious how the shoeing went with the old dude horses.

"Frank, how did that shoeing work out with the dude horses?"

He walked over to be away from the other people and said, "Doc, you ruined my reputation."

"What are you talking about?" I asked.

"Doc, people are saying that Frank is so stupid, he doesn't know which direction to put shoes on a horse."

45

R ainbow Bear

Saturday night. It's been a long week of caring for farm and ranch animals. We're having some friends over for a potluck, drinking too.

The phone rings. I have to answer, of course, as I'm the only vet around for farm animals.

I pick up the phone and say, "Hello."

"Are you the vet?" he asks.

"Yes. Who is this?" I reply.

"Rainbow Bear," he answers.

After a few drinks I'm feeling a bit cheeky and reply, "Rainbow bear-where did that name come from?"

Then he tells me. He's living with a group of people in teepees somewhere in the southern part of the state.

"We live close to nature and take animal and nature names."

I ask him why he is calling. He tells me that he is visiting friends nearby and has a problem.

"I just went out to the garbage can in the backyard to dump some trash. There's a possum by the garbage can. It's sick, maybe even dead. No, I could see it move a tiny bit. Maybe it's dying though. I don't know what to do."

"It's playing possum," I tell him.

"What?" he replies.

Then I explain it: When possums are frightened, they play dead. It's a protective behavior, a survival mechanism so they will be left alone. It's called "playing possum".

"Leave it alone but go back in 30 minutes or so. It should be gone."

"Really?" He's flabbergasted by all this.

"Call me back in a half an hour and let me know, ok?" I ask.

"Ok," he replies with definite skepticism.

Later he calls back and tells me the possum has disappeared.

46

Hardscrabble Acres

I.

About Charley.

He was middle aged of a short, stocky built. Disheveled is another word that works. His humor ranged from dry to cynical.

He moved from Ohio with his wife Kathy.

They had a small diary along the Columbia River and maybe milked 20-30 cows. And he always had a scruffy bull. The farm was like him, disheveled. Actually, it was a mess. He knew it and called it Hardscrabble Acres. In fact, he had a magnetic metal sign on his old pickup that read, Hardscrabble Acres. He was proud of that.

A couple more things.

He had been in World War II. Maybe in Europe. During the war he learned to fly airplanes.

I have since thought he sought a secluded, peaceful place after his war experience. However, he didn't say much about it.

One summer he showed up with a small airplane, probably a war leftover. It was small and light but could carry two people. That was pretty cozy though. It had an enormous wing and a very small engine, probably like a large lawnmower of today. He kept it behind the barn and used the pasture for a runway. Because it was so light and had such a large wing surface, it was airborne quickly.

It wasn't long before he came up with a part time job for him and the airplane. It was summer and there were worries of forest fires.

He flew over the lower part of the river, over both Washington and Oregon looking for fires. He also ranged into the big valley south of Portland.

The valley presented a problem though. It got hot there, unlike along the lower river near the coast. For some reason he had to make stops in the valley. I'm not sure why, maybe that's where he picked up the spotter that flew with him.

If it got too hot and it was a black asphalt landing strip, summer heat coming back up from the asphalt created strong upward currents of air. He couldn't land because the enormous wings and the lightness of the plane caused it to be pushed away from the landing strip. He had to find another place to land or just wait it out.

In the long run, actually it was a short run, he lost his job. It was a cozy airplane and he just too friendly with his spotters who were all young women.

2.

     "Doc, you won't believe this about my bull."

"What about your bull?"

"He's been gone several weeks. I figured he drowned in the slough."

Charley usually kept a bull around, but I didn't pay much attention. I did know his fencing was pretty lousy as it was loosely hung barbed wire. It kept the cows in as they usually didn't have much wanderlust. Bulls were a different story; they liked to go visiting.

"He got tangled in the fence and castrated himself. It's crazy. Come see him."

"Okay, I can be there in an hour or so."

MONTY WAS EXCITED, even distraught. He was checking a pasture full of his prized purebred Jersey heifers. They were now just old enough to breed. When he arrived, he discovered a very scruffy Holstein bull with them.

"You've got to come help. I can't let him breed my purebred heifers," he explained.

I left and was there in 20 minutes. Sure enough, among the heifers was a forlorn, scruffy bull. Fortunately, he was gentle. I roped him and tied him to a tree. The tree was on the edge of the pasture that bordered State Forest lands.

"Find out who owns the bull. We can leave him tied for the time being," I said. "Let me know and I'll come back later to help if you need me."

There were no cellphones in those days, so it took a while going house to house. It took quite a while, but no luck.

Monty called me and I went back to help him. We had a dilemma. A pasture of ready to breed purebred heifers and a stray bull with no owner that could be found.

We knew what needed to be done. We didn't even need

to talk about it. Anyway, the bull wasn't that big or rowdy, and Monty was an ex college football lineman. It was a pretty even match, actually.

He restrained the bull. I performed the procedure. He was now a steer and couldn't breed anything. We turned him loose and chased him into the forest.

All that was several weeks before Charley called about arrival of his missing bull. The bull had made a round trip of 8 miles, swam several sloughs and gone through a lot of fences.

Charley was happy his bull, rather steer, was back. He wasn't very concerned about "surgery". After all, it wasn't much of a bull to start with. Anyway, he could fatten it up and butcher it for meat later.

I think what he liked best was a new story to tell people. He liked his story so much I didn't try to dissuade him.

3.

In those days I drove a lot of miles and covered a lot of counties. Usually, I stopped for lunch at a small cafe midway between all my work. It was a stopping place for other guys working about the country. It those days it was mostly guys too. Plumbers, electricians, builders, repairmen. I knew most of them because we all lived in the same community. Anyway, a lot of them had a few cows, or raised pigs, or maybe their wife or daughter had a horse.

Most had their own business, so we had that in common too.

"How's business?" "Keeping busy?" "How is your new help working out?" was our typical conversation.

Or maybe about sports, or hunting, or fishing.

Maybe, the most important question was: "Do you have

any problem getting money out of old man Johnson?" Or whoever.

Since we all knocked on doors, there was another thing that came up. It was sort of a quiet fantasy that we all harbored. It was this: we knocked on the door and a naked woman answered.

Charley called. He had a sick cow. I set up a time to meet him at his barn.

I arrived in an hour or so. I looked around but couldn't find him or a cow. I called out, no response. He didn't seem to be in the field either.

Finally, I walked up the house, which wasn't far. I knocked on the door. No response. I knocked again. Again, no response. It seemed like I heard something though. I waited, then knocked again.

Finally, the door opened. There was his wife, stark naked. "Oh, I thought you were Charley," she said.

I was dumbfounded. Not that I minded seeing a naked woman. After all, that was a common, but rarely discussed, fantasy of men who knock on doors for a living. But, as sweet as she was, Kathy wasn't on the fantasy list. Let's just say she had spent too many years indulging in irresistible dairy products. I'll leave it at that.

Before I could even think about it, I said, "Kathy, put your clothes on."

I finally found Charley. We took care of his cow. As I was leaving, I said, "I think you should go to the house, your wife is expecting you."

R einhold Stories

I.

Reinhold grew up in the eastern part of Germany, the part that became East Germany after the war. The family of father, mother, two sisters and Reinhold lived on a family farm in a small valley. They lived in a house built in the 1300's. It was still the old days there. They farmed with horses, no tractors and they rarely traveled far. In fact, he told me you could tell people from a different valley because they spoke just a little differently with a slight accent. They raised crops and had horses, cattle, sheep and, of course, chickens. His mother and sisters always had a large garden. Reinhold worked with the horses a lot. He had fond memories of the horses because life could only go as fast as the horses. Reinhold and his sisters went to school but only through 8 grades.

Then the war came and everything changed, forever. His father was conscripted into the army and sent to the Eastern Front. The government sent prisoners of war from Russia to help on the farm.

At some point his father contracted tuberculosis and was taken off the front lines. His doctor sent him to the barracks for rest and possible cure. One day, two officers found him resting and branded him a traitor which was punishable by death at that time. They bound his arms and took him behind the barracks for execution.

He was on the ground on his knees and head down for the execution. At that moment his doctor walked by and confronted the officers.

He was outraged and told them the man was very ill with tuberculosis and was in the barracks convalescing under his orders.

Reinhold's father was saved and not too long later he was sent home to heal.

Near the end of the war, the Americans overtook their area. Unfortunately, this area had been given previously to Russia in an early agreement. Soon the Russians were in charge of life in Reinhold's community.

Everything changed. Land and buildings were taken away and local lickspittles were put in charge.

Finally, Reinhold's father gathered up the family and left. They traveled to Berlin and they were able to escape to the west side of the city that was occupied by the Allies.

2.

Eventually, Reinhold ended up with a small farm in a valley along our big river. Not too surprisingly as he was industrious, ambitious and hard working. He worked at another job too. So, two jobs.

His farm was a small dairy. Cows to milk, young to raise, hay to make. A lot to do.

Mixed in all that was a young man with, well, all the normal young man interests.

He needed some help especially with the young animals. It has always seemed women understand young animals better than men.

Helen lived at the end of the road. She was married to an older guy who was gone almost all the time driving his big truck across the country. Actually, he was gone all the time. She was bored. Reinhold hired her to feed and care for the calves and other young stock.

They got to know each other and had something in common. They were lonely.

One evening, late in the fall when the rains had started and it was getting colder, Reinhold invited her into his house for a drink to warm up before going home.

Well, as it turns out she didn't go home. That was just fine for both of them. They needed a reprieve from their loneliness.

It was just fine until very early hour the next morning when they begin to hear sirens. The firetrucks with their sirens went right past Reinhold's to the end of the road to Helen's house. It burned to the ground.

I didn't hear the rest of the story, so I'm not sure how they worked things out.

3.

Reinhold hardly stood still, he was ambitious. He kept buying more farmland and building bigger dairies. After a number of years, he had lots of land and a large diary on a hill with considerable farm land surrounding it.

He also found Shirley, they got married and soon had

two kids. Reinhold now had extra land to sell after all his acquisitions.

That's where Ed and I come in. We met at the university and became good, very good, friends. He was an animal science major and I, of course, a vet.

One of our far-fetched dreams was to buy a ranch in Oregon, the central or eastern part. We would scour the advertisements. For $100,000 it seemed like we could buy a small working cattle ranch. He would run it. I'd bet a vet on the side and my wife would teach school to help pay for things. He would need a schoolteacher wife eventually too.

Well, none of it worked. We would go look at these ranches and realize it would take 4 people working full time somewhere else to support the ranch and pay for it.

Then I was introduced to northwestern Oregon by rancher I knew quite well in California.

While visiting and considering moving there, I learned Reinhold had farmland to sell.

I told Ed about this, and we traveled north to meet Reinhold and talk about buying land. However, we did not want to be known as Californians, those people with ridiculous amounts of money and thus commanding higher prices. Our solution was to be two schoolteachers from Prineville, in central Oregon. We figured we couldn't possibly be rich as schoolteachers.

Ed and I had looked over the lands for sale and were now in Reinhold's living room having drinks and talking about prices. He was shrewd, but we figured he wouldn't be at this point in life if he wasn't.

Regardless, we were enjoying ourselves, drinking and bargaining.

Then Shirley walked in to join us. She was quite curious

about our origins. We told her we were schoolteachers from Prineville.

"I grew up in Prineville," she immediately responded.

I looked Ed, "This is going to be a problem," I thought. He was thinking the same thing.

After a few more questions from her. Then there were a couple of quite specific questions that we could not possibly answer. Ed and I looked at each other,we knew the gig was up.

Ed then explained all about us. We had more drinks and ended up not only buying land but becoming lifelong friends. Of course, they never let us forget our faux Prineville origins.

4.

"You gotta come, now there's been accident!" Shirley was frantic.

"Reinhold took one of the horses to go check heifers in the back field. Something happened, they ended up in the slough. Come quick!"

Horses falling into sloughs are a scary thing. They could break legs, cut them open, or puncture their chest or abdomen in the murky water. Often old branches or even trees could be hidden under water.

I hurried down to their farm along the big river.

When I arrived, the first thing I saw was the horse tied to the fence below the house. Except for very muddy legs, it was quiet, and I quickly discovered no injuries. I was perplexed.

Shirley called out from the house, "Up here, come to the house."

Now I was really perplexed.I walked to the house

quickly. "The horse looks fine," I said more as a question than anything.

"It's not the horse. It's Reinhold."

She led me to the bedroom where Reinhold lay in their bed. He was semiconscious and moaning. I was startled and pretty scared by what I saw. Obviously, he had hit his head and now had a significant concussion and maybe more. This was definitely out of my league

"I called you because you are the nearest medical help," she explained. "Please help him."

Obviously veterinarians are not trained to handle human head injuries, but we do have insight to something serious.

"Call an ambulance and do it right now. This could be serious," I replied. "He needs to get to the hospital as soon as possible."

She did, he went to the hospital for a couple days and then was back farming.

That wasn't the last time I sent somebody to their doctor or the hospital after listening to their health conditions.

5.

George drove a supply truck. He visited all the farms. The dairies mainly.

They needed lots of supplies: parts for milking machines, soaps and disinfectants to keep things clean, rubber mats for the milkers to stand on, rubber boots and thick socks, rain suits, knitted hats and gloves, medicines for the cows and some tools too.

Plus, they needed new gadgets. Everybody loved a new gadget as maybe it would make life easier.

This time George had a nylon webbing apparatus to use

when a cow couldn't deliver a calf. It was composed of nylon webbing and a couple metal rings. You could strap yourself in the webbing and then use the extensions with the metal rings to make loops to put around the calf's feet. Then you just leaned back and helped deliver the calf.

This would be fine with dairy cows. They're used to people and very quiet to be around. That wouldn't be true with beef cows, particularity those on the range.

Reinhold thought this was really a good idea. He could keep it in his pocket when checking his cows, use if needed, and simply hose it clean when finished. He used it a couple times and it worked well.

One day, while touring his barn and checking out his cows, he found a cow that needed help. She was calving and the calf's two front feet were out as well as the nose.

He thought that this situation would be perfect for his gadget. He strapped himself in, made loops with the rings and attached them to the calf's feet. Reinhold leaned back to help the cow and speed the delivery.

Suddenly, the cow got up started running away. Reinhold was trapped in the webbing. He tried to run fast enough to keep up with cow. However, that only scared her and she ran more. Finally, he fell and after being dragged though copious amounts of manure, the cow stopped. She was probably exhausted at this point. Reinhold got his knife and cut himself free.

That was the last time he used that gadget, and he didn't buy a new one either.

48

The Heart Attack Dilemma

BEVERLY RAISED all kinds of exotic animals. She could raise and care for almost anything. Once she raised a clutch of abandoned baby flickers. My biologist friends had never heard of that one.

One day, I bought a hedgehog from her and gave it to my daughter when she was at college. Cutest little thing in the world. Except, it was up all night. Turns out they are nocturnal and just as bad, their poop is the worst smelling in the animal kingdom. Not an ideal apartment pet.

Of course, someone had to sponsor Beverly's animals, and that was her husband, Robert.

Robert was late middle age, but it was really hard to tell. He always looked the worse for wear and was smoking, coughing and breathing too hard. He was overweight and only drank enough alcohol so he could keep working.

Haggard and potbellied, but quick witted and quick with a quote.

For work, he was a masterful builder of large ocean fishing nets. He was considered the best. His nets were creative and the best built. He had an amazing, widespread reputation.

I cared for Beverly's miniature horses and donkeys, and various obscure breeds of sheep and goats she collected and from which she raised offspring..

One day I was caring for one Beverly's exotics, maybe a miniature donkey. Robert stopped by to visit, which he often did when I was there.

He looked as haggard as ever. In spite of that, I still asked how things were going.

"I had a heart attack a couple months ago. I just went to my doctor and got some new restrictions."

I was really bothered. I knew he never looked that good anyway, but a heart attack. That took everything to a different level. Anyway, he still had a cigarette in his mouth, so I doubted he was going to change his ways much.

I stopped what I was doing. "I'm really sorry," I said really concerned.

"What did your doctor tell you?" I asked.

"Well, he said I had to cut out half my sex life."

Now, I was really concerned and worried for him.

Then he continued. "I don't know which half to cut out, thinking about it, or talking about it," he dead panned.

Whether any of it was true, at least he hadn't lost his sense of humor.

49

Rosie

HE JUST APPEARED ONE AFTERNOON. I didn't know him. In fact, I still don't know his name even many years later.

"I need your help."

"What's going on?" I answered.

"It's Rosie, she needs your help."

"Who is Rosie?" I asked.

"An elk, she's in my backyard. She won't leave and has been eating my wife's rose bushes. She needs a vet," he replied.

"You need to contact Fish and Wildlife," I answered.

"I did. They told me to leave her alone and let nature take its course. I think she needs a shot, like penicillin or something," he said.

This was a tricky area for me and other vets— treating

wild animals. There's both legality and morality. That's not even including how you safely deal with a very large, wild animal.

Struggling with the dilemma, I finally asked, "Where do you live?"

It turned out he lived about a mile away in cluster of houses, a country subdivision of sorts

"I'll follow you and take a look. No promises though, I'm not legally allowed to treat wild animals like this."

I followed him to his house in my pickup.

He led me to the backyard where the elk Rosie was staying.

She sat quietly, chewing her cud. She was a bit skinny, scruffy too but alert. I walked around her but not too close so as to not disturb her. She had two very large wounds on both sides of her abdomen. They had been there for a while. One was draining pus, obviously infected.

"She's really quiet. I think you can just give her a shot," he was almost pleading.

I was thinking, thinking hard. "Could I really do this? Successfully?

"Or was this going to be another near-death experience for me?"

"I have a very long-acting drug, kind of like penicillin. It will last for a week. It won't sting either. But the needle, if she doesn't like the needle, well it won't work," I told him.

"Please try it."

I calculated the dosage and loaded my syringe. I needed a large needle to get the drug injected quickly, but not too big to startle and send her running.

I approached her slowly, talking to her to whole time. I'm not sure if I was reassuring her or me. Maybe both. She stayed quiet.

I stuck the large needle in a rear leg. She barely moved. I connected the syringe. She stayed quiet. I injected the antibiotic as quick as possible. She still didn't move.

A few days later, she left the yard. Both of us wanted to believe she got better though we'll never know.

50

S aying Hello

IT HAD BEEN A LONG, very long summer day. I had been traveling the back roads visiting farms and ranches taking care of difficult horses, and wild cattle. I was exhausted.

It was near dark already when I stopped at a small store with a gas station. My truck needed gas.

I started the gas pump, put the nozzle in my gas tank and went to the small restroom on the side of the store.

As I finished and was washing up, a young man entered. He was wind blown, sunburned, dirty, and as it turns out angry, probably at the world.

"Do you want to fight?"

All at once a lot of things were going through my mind or trying too. I was surprised, shocked, maybe even a little scared. But really, I was just tired.

"I'm too tired," I finally replied without really thinking things through.

"Me too," was his answer.

He immediately relaxed, the anger disappeared, and we began to talk. What a relief for both of us.

It turns out he had spent the last two days hitchhiking across several states to find and visit his grandmother.

I finished gassing up my truck and bought him a soda, some chips and a sandwich. He had no money left and hadn't eaten since the day before.

I took him with me, maybe ten miles or so to another road he needed to be on. We didn't say much. I think we were both tired and wanted to be lost in our own thoughts.

I stopped at the turnoff. He started to get out.

I said, "Hey, next time say hello first. Ok?"

He looked at me nodded and grunted an answer and was gone.

I didn't even know his name, but I hoped he would find his grandmother and his life would work out.

51

S OS*

*SAVE our Salmon

Bernard and his wife had moved from the east coast a couple of years before. They had lived in a large city, maybe Baltimore. I'm not sure. He had worked for the city in planning. The kids were gone, and they were ready for a change.

He found a job in a small coastal town that was beginning to see a lot of change. They needed a new planner. It was perfect for everybody.

They found a couple of secluded acres where they put up a modular house and he built a barn. He wanted some animals. Eventually, he got a couple donkeys, several goats and, like everybody else in the country, chickens.

A small creek ran through the property. It was well fed by a number of springs and always had water in it. This little creek emptied into a fairly good-sized river known for its salmon runs.

Unknown to Bernard, his little creek was a perfect spawning creek for Silver, or Coho salmon. The fish were the right size for it, not too big. He also didn't know much about salmon and their spawning habits.

It was fall, and the spawning season had started. Fish were migrating out of the ocean, up bigger rivers. Eventually, they would return to the smaller creeks where they were born. There they would pair up and spawn.

One fall day, Bernard was exploring his new creek. It was still all new to him, as he hadn't been there long. Suddenly, he discovered two salmon in an open area on the creek. That spot was filled with small gravel. They fish seemed to be trouble by the way they moved. He thought that maybe they were trapped and maybe they came the wrong way. That was his thinking.

Furthermore, maybe they needed his help. He figured he needed to catch them and return them to the river where they belong.

He built a dam below them and above them. It wasn't hard because the creek became very narrow in those places. Then he caught each salmon. I'm not sure how he did that. That wasn't easy. They are quick and strong. Finally, he got them into a couple of big buckets and put lids on them to keep them from jumping out.

He took the buckets with fish to his pickup, drove to the big river and released them. He was convinced he saved the lost fish.

Unfortunately, the fish had to again find their home creek and make another run for spawning.

The Arm

GLADYS STILL LIVED in the old family farmhouse. She had spent her whole life there and inherited it from her father along with the farmland. The land now belonged to her son who ran several hundred head of black Angus beef cows.

Gladys had been widowed for years and lived alone except for her two dogs, one large and one small. She was a bit of a recluse, if not eccentric. Everybody knew it and she knew it too.

The old house was along the county road and near the Columbia River. Every morning, she took the two dogs, the large one and the small one, on a long walk. They crossed the road, walked through the cottonwood trees to a large sandy beach. This occurred almost every day, unless the weather was really terrible.

It was usually very private in the early mornings and

there was always something to see; fishing boats, large cargo ships, deer, flotsam. You never knew what might wash up. The dogs loved running the beach too.

One very typical morning, the dogs were running out ahead of her when they suddenly stopped. The small one turned and ran back to Gladys as fast as it could. The large dog had stopped before something that had washed up and was barking ferociously. It looked like a log to Gladys.

She walked up to it. The small dog stayed well behind her. The big dog kept barking.

As she got there, she suddenly realized it was a human body and by the looks of it, dead for some time.

"I've got to report this," she said to herself. "Maybe I'll go to my neighbor."

She thought more. "That won't work, my neighbors think I'm too strange to believe me."

She walked around the badly decomposing body trying to decide what to do. Then she saw one arm was almost detached. "Maybe they'll believe it I take it with me for proof," she thought.

Gladys took off her scarf and used it to grab the arm. It came apart easily and off she went to her neighbors.

The small dog stayed well behind, but she had to keep the big dog from grabbing the arm.

The neighbors certainly believed her about the body but were more certain than ever that she was just plain strange.

The Errant Bull

"Doc!" There was a urgency in his voice. Gary was an experienced rancher. He ran lots, maybe thousands, of cattle. He leased many small farms over several counties and two states. Most things didn't bother him, but this one did.

"What's going on?" I asked.

He proceeded to explain that an unknown black bull showed up at one of his places. He had horns too. Gary's farm was full of virgin purebred heifers that he was raising for a wealthy rancher from the eastern part of the state. They were old enough to breed, but not to this roaming bull.

Gary and his cowboys tried to drive the bull out through the broken fence, but it turned on the horses. It wasn't safe to herd him. He did not respect horses and that was dangerous and maybe life threatening to the horses and their riders.

"We can't get very close to him, or he will charge our horses. Right now, he's mixed with the heifers, probably deciding which ones to breed. We have to do something."

Like a lot of ranchers, Gary had a dart gun. Most of the small farms he leased had lousy fences. In fact, they would only work if there was enough grass inside the fence to feed the cattle. They had no facilities for handling the cattle.

So, unless a portable system was brought in, a dart gun was the logical choice, especially if time was a concern. Sick animals could be darted with a syringe of antibiotics. Most of the newer drugs lasted several days or more, so it was often a one-shot treatment.

I had set most of the ranchers up with a tranquilizer they could use in their dart guns. Sometimes they needed a sedate animal to handle, like when delivering a calf.

The ranchers and their cowboys were good shots, actually amazing shots. Since they all hunted deer and elk, that's not surprising. Occasionally, I would hire one to come with me to sedate an animal that was uncatchable but needed treatment.

"I'm thinking I should shoot him with the tranquilizer I got from you. Then we could decide what to do with him. How much should I use?" he asked.

I gave him a dosage.

"Can you get close enough?"

"I think so, I'll have to go by foot. He'll charge a horse if he sees one."

"That sounds dangerous. Be careful."

"He's pretty busy with the heifers, so I think it will work." Then Gary hung up.

Several hours later Gary called back.

"I got close enough to shoot him, a good shot in his rump, but it spooked him, and he took off running. He ran through two more fences came to a big slough and started to swim across it. About halfway across the tranquilizer set in. His head dropped into the water, and he drowned."

Then he called back a bit later. "Can we butcher the bull to feed the dogs?" he asked

They had a lot of cattle dogs. Good dogs too. It's amazing how important a good herding dog is to a cattleman.

I thought about it and replied, "I don't think you should use the bull for dog food. That's a potent drug in his flesh. Get your backhoe and bury him instead. You don't want other animals getting into him either."

I don't think he ever discovered who owned the bull or even where he came from. Maybe the owner was glad he disappeared too. It wasn't a nice animal. Very dangerous in fact.

54

All Fall Down

GARY CALLED back a few days later.

"Doc, I talked to the owner of those purebred heifers. He wants me to abort them."

"Good idea," I replied. "But you need to wait a week or so after the bull has been gone."

He already had the drug. Because of his far-reaching operation, I had set him up with a lot of treatments to have on hand for all sorts of problems.

"OK, I'll wait a bit and then have my guys do it," he answered.

About a week later Gary called back. He was really alarmed, worse than about the errant bull.

"The heifers are getting a reaction to the abortion drug. They walk out of the chute for a little bit and then fall down. There's 8 or 10 laid out flat. I think they're dying."

He was absolutely right to be alarmed. I was too. However, drug reactions are pretty unusual, in fact really rare anymore. This didn't sound like a reaction I would expect to occur. I was a bit stumped.

Finally, out of desperation, I said, "Have your guys look at the label. Let's see what the bottle shows."

It wasn't long before he called back. There were more down, but nobody had died. They just seemed to be sleeping peacefully.

"They were using the tranquilizer for the dart instead of the abortion drug. It's my fault too. That's the bottle I gave them to use."

Actually, that was good news, in fact great news. No weird reaction was happening, and they would sleep it off and be fine.

I told him just that and suggested some things to help the heifers along.

In a couple hours they were all awake and up walking, maybe a bit wobbly, however.

55

The Bull Rider

EVERY COUPLE YEARS or so our county fair would host a bull-riding-only rodeo. They would contract with a rodeo stocker and have 40 or 50 bulls brought in. Usually about that many riders showed up too.

Some of the riders were pros, some weren't. The same with the bulls. It was sort of the B team of bulls and riders. That didn't mean it wasn't fun to watch. It definitely was.

These events always have cowboys, their horses and, of course, the clowns. The cowboys and their horses were first class, as were the clowns. The clowns are always remarkable. They are quick, nimble and brave to the point of being crazy. But they save countless bull riders from harm and maybe even death.

So, it's always a good show between the bulls, the riders, the cowboys and the clowns.

I was always asked to come as the vet in case a bull needed medical attention. I always agreed as I loved the show too. I wasn't very worried about injured bulls. They're too big and strong with most of them weighing 2000-3000 pounds. That's ten to fifteen times bigger than the riders. Plus, they have horns..

By the way, these bulls have a pretty good life. If you've ever thought about being reincarnated as an animal, consider being a rodeo bull. They spend over 99% of their time just eating and lying around chewing their cud in some nice pasture with free medical care too. When it comes to work it's just a several days a week during the rodeo season. Even then, it's in short stints of up to 8 seconds, or less, if you're a good bucking bull. As a consequence, it's a pretty good life.

There are always medical folks for the riders too. Usually, there are a couple EMT's with an ambulance in waiting. After all, it's the bull riders who can and do get hurt in this sport.

I was sitting just above pens where the bulls were loaded, rigged and the riders got on. With me was Bob, an EMT. There was an ambulance just outside.

Things were going pretty smoothly. So far, the bulls had bucked off all the riders. The clowns got the bulls away from the grounded riders and the cowboys on horseback herded the bulls out.

A new bull was loaded in the pen just below us. He was a bit snorty already. More than usual. A rider eased onto him and the assistants got the rigging in place. Then the bull went nuts. It sounded like he was going to tear the whole barn down. There was a lot of yelling and screaming. The screaming was coming from the rider.

Bob was down to the pen in an instant. He wanted to

make sure the rider was ok. The rider assured everybody he was, and to please just turn the bull loose.

The ride lasted about 2 seconds. The rider was down sprawled out on the ground and the bull turned to go after him. A clown was there immediately and diverted the bull. Another clown diverted the bull away from him. Then the cowboys moved in with their horses to herd the bull out.

The rider was still down. He made a feeble attempt but couldn't get up. Bob hopped the fence and ran to the rider. The clowns were there and other riders too. There was lots of help. Soon the ambulance was there and he was put on a stretcher and taken to our local hospital.

Bob returned and sat beside me. "What do you think happened?" I asked.

"I think he got hurt in the pen when the bull was raising hell. Upper leg, I think. X-rays will tell," he replied.

"Will they let you know?"

"Yeah, they'll call as soon as they know." he answered.

The show went on. Riders trying to ride the bulls. The bulls winning every time. Fortunately, nobody or bulls got hurt after that. And the clowns were great.

Bob's phone rang. He answered, talked for a bit, and then hung up. He was shaking his head as he told me the report.

"He broke his femur. That's the biggest bone in the body which you know. I'm sure it happened in the pen, but he rode anyway."

"Are those guys brave or crazy?" I asked.

Bob thought for a moment and said, "I'm pretty sure it's both."

56

B ethany and Scout

BETHANY WAS MAYBE ELEVEN. She was tall for her age, slim with long brown hair that fell to her shoulders. She lived with her parents near the end of the road along a small creek in the southern part of our county. I'm not sure if she had brothers and sisters.

But she had Scout. He was a small horse in his late teens. Probably a pony cross. Maybe part Arab or Morgan. It was hard to tell. He was kind and gentle. Folks in the horse world would say he had a kind eye.

Scout would do anything for Bethany, and that's why I am driving as fast as I can.

Bethany had been riding Scout most of the day on forested roads and trails. Coming home, she decided to lead Scout across a wooden bridge. It was a shortcut. The bridge was strong, made of full sized 4 by 12 timbers. You could drive across it easily. But there were spaces between the timbers, maybe 4-6 inches. Easy enough for a person walking or even a dog. For a horse though, a disaster waiting to happen,

It did too. About halfway across Scout slipped between two of the timbers. In his panic to get free, another foot fell through too. He was now trapped. Now he had his two back legs trapped between the timbers.

It was late in a long summer day. There was still lots of light and the remaining day was warm. I finally arrived at the turn off and started up the road along the small creek.

I wasn't exactly sure where to find Bethany and her horse. Suddenly, it was obvious. There were a lot of people, maybe 20-30 and a fire truck, an emergency response vehicle, two sheriff's cars, and a backhoe. A backhoe? They're good a burying things usually. But maybe lifting too. Two loggers, with big chainsaws too.

They were all waiting for me.

One of the Deputies came forward. "He's down this way," and led me to the bridge. Scout sitting on the bridge with his back legs sticking through the spaces. He was quiet. Bethany and her mother were at his head trying comfort him. Actually, the mother was trying to comfort her daughter who was crying uncontrollably.

I asked people to stay back let me look at Scout alone. I was worried about startling him and causing more damage. I approached him quietly while talking. He seemed willing to just sit there and not struggle. Slowly I examined him as much as possible. I didn't want to trigger a reaction from him. He stayed quiet during my exam. I talked to him, so did Bethany's mother. Bethany could only cry.

"She says it's her fault, and he's going to have broken legs and need to be put down," her mother lamented.

I couldn't tell for sure, but I only found some small cuts and abrasions. No broken legs that I could detect. I told mother and daughter of my findings but cautioned them.

I needed and plan and I needed it fast.

I went back to the waiting crowd and explained my quickly devised plan.

I told them that he seemed ok considering what happened, but things could unravel easily. The bridge needed to be cut away from his hind legs, but the chainsaws would scare him and that could cause more damage.

I would give a couple IV drugs to put him to sleep. We would have about 30 minutes to work. We would wrap a towel around his head to protect his eyes and help keep him quiet.

The loggers with chainsaws would go to work as soon as I gave the word. Once the wood was removed, we could haul him up and free him by his tail. A couple of strong men could do that. There were more than a few available. I would direct everybody.

We needed a big, strong tarp. There was one in the emergency response vehicle. Once Scout was free from the bridge, we would work the tarp under him. Then he could be moved off the bridge to a slightly sloped grassy area nearby. We would pull the tarp to move him. There was lots of help for that. Then the tarp could be removed, and I could examine Scout more carefully and treat him as needed.

The loggers were quick and we pulled him free, put him on the tarp, and suddenly he was laying on a safe grassy spot. We removed the tarp. I looked him over carefully, very carefully. Surprisingly, and pleasantly so, he had no serious injuries. Especially no broken legs. I treated him with some drugs for pain and possible infection.

I asked the people to move away and be quiet so not to disturb his recovery. It was then I noticed Bethany. She was up a bit further, head buried in the grass crying. I wasn't ready to declare the horse fine just yet.

An experienced horseman stayed at his head. She had worked with me before and knew what to do. I positioned myself at his tail. Scout stayed asleep about another 15 minutes and then begin to stir. We took the towel off his head. Finally, he rolled up and stayed that way for a short while. Then as horses do, put his front legs out. He was ready to get up. He struggled briefly and was then up, but very unsteady. The woman at his head steadied him there. I used the tail to do likewise.

This was going to be the critical moment, was he ok or not? He shifted his weight back and forth staggering some as he was still not sure of his balance, or just what worked in his legs.

Suddenly, he steadied himself. All the legs worked. He could stand on all of them. Scout would be fine.

Everybody sighed in relief and congratulations of a job well done spread quickly. The woman holding his head said she would take him home for the night, or longer.

"Don't put him in a stall, keep him a small corral or pen. He needs to move around, or he'll stiffen up," I recommended. She understood and agreed.

People began to disappear. It was evening now and would be dark soon.

Suddenly, Bethany ran up, threw her arms around me, and started crying again. Her whole body shook. I pulled back and looked at her.

"He going to be fine," I said.

"I know, I'm crying because I'm happy this time," she replied.

She put her head back against me. I could smell the summer grasses and small flowers in her hair. I held her as long as she wanted.

57

The Doeling

IT WAS LATER in the spring, maybe May. The world was green from the spring rains and now warm days. It had been a long day for me out on the farms.

I was returning on a backcountry, rural road lost in my thoughts. As I came around a curve I found a young deer in the road before me. She had been stuck by another vehicle, maybe a truck. She lunged before me and off the road. Her rear legs were severely damaged. She couldn't use them at all.

I drove to a small turn around and returned. She now was in the grass below the road. One back leg dangled behind her. It was almost completely severed.

Slowly I walked toward her, not sure what to do. As I approached, she screamed and lunged forward using her front legs. The back legs were useless.

I had no idea deer could scream. She was terrified, she was horribly injured, and she was in immense pain.

I got down on the ground and began talking to her. She became quiet. I kept talking and moved to her. I moved her maimed and dangling leg to where it belonged. For dignity, of course, as it would never heal. I ran my hands over her body, her maimed body. I kept talking, she stayed quiet.

Finally, I realized there was only one thing to be done. I needed to relieve her hopeless suffering. I didn't think I could do this alone, however.

There was a house nearby. Nobody was home.

A car came by and stopped. I explained the problem to the woman driving and. I asked for help. She fled. "I can't really blame her," I thought.

I would have to do this alone.

In my truck I kept a solution for horrible and hopeless situations. I brought it out. I filled a syringe with it

As I approached, the young deer screamed and lunged away. Again, I got down on my knees and crawled towards her. I talked to her the whole time. Again, she quieted.

I found her large neck vein. I kept talking. She stayed quiet as I injected my drug.

A small breeze came up. Then it was gone.

The young deer laid as quietly and peaceful as the grasses around her.

The Gift of Clumsiness

TWO BROTHERS. One normal, fisherman in our big river in the fall and Alaska in the summer. The other clumsy, both in mind and body.

We need the clumsy one. Only he knows where the cow is this stormy night, somewhere below in a flooded field.

I was actually on my way to the annual cattlemen's dinner where a piece of excellent prime rib, some drinks and good visits awaited. Instead, I'll be out in a February storm to deliver a calf.

We meet at their barn. I don rain gear and high rubber boots and gather what gear I may need.

Then we are off into the night with only flashlights to help, and the clumsy brother who can find the cow. He falls, gets up and apologizes.

"I'm just a clumsy guy," he tells us. His brother issues an

age-old criticism about the clumsiness. This has probably gone on for twenty years or more.

We continue into the darkness where the field is filled with swamp grass and water. He continues to fall. "He truly is clumsy," I decided. His brother continues to criticize. I say nothing.

Finally, we reach the cow. She's young, a heifer. It's probably her first calf. She's not very big either so that makes the situation worse.

We need to move her out of the water, at least a little. There are three of us and she's small, so it's not that hard.

The fisherman brother holds her head. The young heifer is content lying in his arms. The clumsy brother holds both flashlights.

I begin my work. The calf has just started to come out. There are two hooves, one slightly ahead of the other, and the nose just behind. That's normal, but the heifer is exhausted and has given up.

I attach my chains above the hooves, hook handles to the chains and pull. First one foot. Then the other. Then the head is out, and the calf takes a breath. It's alive and I'm surprised.

I pull hard, the calf is suddenly out and into the water beside me. It can drown.

The clumsy brother drops the flashlights and goes into the water. He comes up holding the calf to his chest. He has saved the calf's life. We move it to its mother near her head. She immediately begins to lick it dry. Things should be alright now.

We find the flashlights and start our journey back.

The clumsy brother falls again. This time his brother helps him up and says, "You did good tonight, David. You did good."

The Google Game

THE PHONE'S RINGING. It's 2 AM. I need to answer it. People don't call at this hour unless it's important.

Maybe a mare is trying to have a foal. Or maybe a cow had a calf, and her uterus came out too and it's all over the ground.

Or maybe, heaven forbid, a horse got on the highway and was struck by a car. These accidents are terrible and the horses are almost always too maimed to survive. But even worse, if the horse goes over the hood and through the windshield, then the people die too.

I answer, very sleepily, "Hello."

"I found a cat," A young woman answers.

"A cat?" I respond still sleepy and now astounded.

She found it along a country road going home late from work. It was off the road in a small turn out. She went back and caught it. That wasn't really difficult. It was young, abandoned and scared.

She was holding it as she talked to me. It was so happy I could hear it purring.

We talked for a while. I told her I was a farm vet but gave her some guidelines which basically were that you have a new friend, take it home and take care of it.

Actually, I was curious about how she found my number. I had been here 30 years or so. I no longer advertised. I no longer used the yellow pages, which were pretty much obsolete at this point. Anyway, she was on a back country road.

"I found you using Google on my phone. Everybody else came up as a vet hospital. You came up alone, so I called you."

That ended well especially for the young cat. Except I could never go back to sleep after something like that, as minor as that was. I needed to look into my listing with Google.

A couple days later, I did a search for vets in my area. Sure enough, there I was listed with all the dog and cat hospitals. There was nothing about this listing that conveyed I was a farm vet only.

I searched the site as well as I could but couldn't figure out how to change my listing or even get rid of it. I closed it and forgot about the whole situation. I had lots of other things to do anyway.

As time went on, the middle of the night dog or cat problem calls kept happening. It was becoming a problem. I often couldn't help people, and it was disturbing my sleep. It was a lose-lose situation.

I went back to the Google and explored it again. I found a way this time. They have a place to rate your experience. I had no ratings at the moment. Most of the dog and cat hospitals had high ratings, like 4-5 out of 5.

Now I had a solution. I concocted a plan. Every week, for a month or so, I would rate myself. I always gave myself the worst rating— a 1. Then I would leave a comment. Most of the comments were very negative. I was hoping it would discourage people from calling me.

The calls didn't really stop, but they slowed down. I think if you're desperate you want a voice, somebody to talk to, in spite of their ratings.

60

The New Family Tree

I HAD his horse's foot in my grasp and was carving an infection out of its hoof.

We were talking, as usual, about all kinds of things.

Lenard was a timber faller. He cut down big trees for a living.

It's one of the most dangerous jobs in the world. He got up very early every morning, cut down trees until mid-day. It took pretty terrible weather to stop his work. Usually, heavy winds would do it.

I asked him more about his work, who he worked with, things like that.

"I work with one of your relatives."

"What?" I was completely confused. I had a wife, a daughter and a son, but no other relatives for 500 miles. None of them fell trees, I knew that for sure.

"Brian," he said.

I kept carving, thinking too. Then I realized that in small communities, there was a different definition of relatives and sometimes blood had very little to do with it. Finally, I said, "You're right, Brian."

Here's how Brian became my relative. My son's wife's mother's second husband's cousin's son was Brian.

Let me repeat that. My son's wife's mother's second husband's cousin's son was Brian.

All in the family.

Maybe it's good we have so many relatives because we can look out for each other and not gossip so much.

Well, maybe that's not true about the gossip.

61

The Shed

LIKE MOST MINK FARMERS, Arne kept a small herd of cattle around.

They were used to graze between the mink barns to keep the weeds and grass down. Besides, it gave the family and the help some meat to eat in the fall.

A typical herd would be two or three or four cows, their calves and a bull. They would be a mixture of many breeds and really hard to tell what. The best thing is that they were very gentle. Anyone could put a rope around their necks and with a bit of pulling and shoving move them anywhere. Even the bulls were gentle, surprisingly.

One night Arne called. He had a young cow with problems having her calf and she needed help.

Naturally, it was raining and a cold, wet evening.

"Can you get a hold of her and put her in one of your sheds out of the rain?" I asked.

"I'll have her waiting for you," he replied.

I arrived about 30 minutes later. Arne had the cow tied in a shed as I asked. She was quietly waiting for me. Unfortunately, the shed was only as long as the cow. Furthermore, the roof sloped to just above where the cow's rear end was. The cow had a wonderful shelter for the birth. However, not only did I have to stand in the rain but all the rain from the roof drained onto me.

I worked as fast as I could to deliver the calf. That was successful as it was a lively, healthy calf. Unfortunately, I was completely soaked from head to foot. I would have been less wet just standing in the rain.

Next time I would definitely ask how long the shed was.

62

Bob Stories

I.

He wasn't young when I met him, but a lot more beat up than he should have been.

A big man, big bones, enormous hands. Tall, but now stooped, hard of breath and he shuffled more than he walked. He wore unlaced tennis shoes because of swollen feet. He always had a cigarette in his mouth.

None the less, Bob had a quick wit, a dry sense of humor and a mischievous twinkle in his eyes. It was hard not to like him, unless he owed you money. He didn't, but it was slow coming sometimes.

In the past, Bob had been a remarkably successful rancher running large numbers of cattle and sheep.

Sometime not too many years past, he found a new partner. Whiskey and more whiskey, and more. This led to money problems, legal problems, some jail time too.

By the time I knew him he wasn't a broken man, but close. He was too big to really break. He was just badly beat up. Bob still had some livestock, small herds of cattle here and there and a flock of sheep where he lived on the island.

He drove an old pickup with metal racks in the back that would hold a cow or some sheep. He always had a helper, but not much of one, who was probably lured by the whiskey.

One day he showed up at my office. He didn't call, just showed up.

Fortunately, I was there with my vet assistant Dan.

This time he had two helpers. As they stumbled around to procure the already down ewe in the back of the pickup I asked, "Why do use these guys?"

"Oh hell, Doc, I hire the handicapped. They're fun to watch."

Finally, they got the ewe onto the ground. She struggled a bit but couldn't stand. I could see this didn't just happen. She looked rough, was very skinny and also heavy in lamb, probably two.

"What's her story?" I asked.

We moved her to a small stall where she could stay and be cared for.

"I found her down about a week ago and figured she would die, but she didn't. So, I brought to you."

"What do you expect me to do?" knowing she was in late pregnancy and near death.

He turned and walked towards his truck. His helpers were already in it. Just as he was ready to get in, he turned and said, "I think a good vet could fix her."

Then he drove away.

We got to work. I took samples, blood and others. Dan ran the lab tests. I treated her for all the things wrong and few that weren't wrong. We made her comfortable and fed her good hay and grain.

Also, we helped her get up and down, like physical therapy for sheep.

It took a while, actually quite a while. A few days later she was eating ok, but it took a couple weeks before she could stand and start filling out.

Then it happened quickly, more weight gain, stronger, getting around well too. Her udder filled with milk.

Then she had two lambs. They were healthy and strong as was she.

I waited a few more days before I called.

"Come get your sheep, they're ready to go," I told him.

It wasn't long before he arrived in his old pickup and just half his motley crew.

As we loaded the ewe and her two lambs, he turned and said, "I knew a good vet could do it."

That was his thank you. But if you think about it, that's a pretty good thank you.

2.

Bob ran a small herd of cows across the county road from our house. About 20 or so and a bull. They were pretty quiet and you didn't see much of them.

In the fall, when he separated the calves to sell it was very noisy for a several days. The calves were calling for their mothers. The cows less so for their calves. Probably at that point they were tired of motherhood. That's what I thought anyway.

One early fall day, he dropped a young bull into the herd.

"What's going on?" I asked. I was surprised and maybe a bit concerned. The old bull was going to consider this an invasion to his territory and probably fight the new bull, maybe hurt it, or even kill it.

"They'll be alright after a few days," he replied rather unconcerned.

The fighting started pretty quickly. It was brutal and noisy. Unfortunately, it was just across the road from our house. This went on several days and nights. If it did stop for a moment, I figured the new bull was dead. But no, no injuries and certainly no fatality.

After two, maybe three more days of fighting, I decided to do something. I loaded my double barreled shotgun with small bird shot and went across the road. I slipped through the fence and approached them warily. They were still fighting and bellowing. Quite frankly, it was frightening, but they completely ignored me.

When I got as close as I felt safe, but probably not really that safe, I shot both bulls in their rumps.

What happened? Nothing! They didn't stop even for a moment. Didn't stop bellowing and didn't stop fighting.

I was stunned and quickly left.

In the end, Bob was right, after a few more days they quit fighting. It was quiet and nobody got hurt.

3.

Bob didn't own the property across the street from us. He leased it from a rather wealthy couple. I suspect they were saving the land to subdivide someday and get even wealthier.

They tolerated the cattle because as a farm they would pay less in taxers.

There was a herd of elk there too. They didn't tolerate the elk however. In truth as majestic and beautiful as they are, elk can be destructive. Like destroying fences.

You would have thought that would have concerned Bob even more. After all he was the one that had to round up escaped cattle and fix the fences. But no, Bob loved the elk. He loved all wild things and was perfectly content to share the land with his cattle.

Finally, the owners had had enough. They contacted the State. The State send biologists to trap and remove the elk. To move them far away to a new home.

The trap was a high sided corral with a one way entrance. No exit. The elk were to be lured by some irresistible treat and thus captured. They could then moved up a chute into trucks to be transported away. It was a well established procedure.

Bob was, well, simply outraged. He thought it was unfair to the elk. And anyway, he liked the animals.

It didn't take him long, he concocted a plan. Bob contacted the Portland Zoo and was soon off to Portland with a pickup full of empty feed sacks. At the zoo he filled the sacks fresh manure from the lions and tigers. Those big animals produce a lot of material daily.

Everyday he spread lion and tiger manure around the entrance to the trap. Of course the elk had never been around or even heard of lions and tigers, but they instinctively knew they could smell a predator.

Bob kept supplying manure as needed. No elk were ever captured. Finally the owners and the State gave up and called the trapping a failure. The trap was dismantled and taken away.

I think Bob the used rest of the manure in his garden.

63

The Last Bob Story

BOB LOVED TO HUNT PHEASANTS, but he loved his dog even more. Both he and his dog were getting old.

After 50 or more years of ranching, Bob was pretty beat up. He couldn't even wear boots anymore, just unlaced tennis shoes. Of course, 50 years of smoking and whiskey didn't help either. He had large, gnarled hands. They looked like old tree roots.

His black lab was even worse off. He had arthritis in his hips and didn't get around very well at all. He was a remarkable hunting dog though. Amazing nose, even today. Maybe that's the last thing to go. I've often wondered. Unlike most retrievers, he would point when he found a pheasant. Naturally, he retrieved too.

I had set Bob up with some drugs to make his dog more comfortable. They helped, but only so much.

Bob bought a bunch of baby pheasants and raised them. They were old enough to turn loose and hunt.

He came by. "I want to hunt my old dog again," he said.

"I thought he was too crippled to hunt." I replied.

"He is now, but I want you to give him something stronger, just for this hunt." He answered.

I thought about it for a bit. "I can set set you up with something powerful, but you can't keep using it." I finally replied. "It's too dangerous to keep using."

I got the drugs together for him and said, "Remember, not too much or too long."

He thanked me, took the drugs and left. I didn't hear from him for a while.

A week or two later, Bob stopped by. He returned almost all the drugs. "That's all you needed?" I asked.

He nodded yes. "I released a bunch of pheasant about a week before. Then I started the drugs, they really worked. He could hunt again. I didn't take him long to find a pheasant. He went on point. He couldn't have been happier. Then I shot him."

64

Too Much Whiskey and Buying Horses

I'M NOT sure about all of his background. As I remember, or was told anyway, he grew up on a ranch in Texas along the Mexican border. He spoke Spanish well, so that made sense. How he ended in Oregon, along the north coast, well, I have no idea.

Jim always had horses: mares, their foals, but usually dude horses to rent for riding on the beach. He would buy the horses at different auctions. Generally, he had a pretty good eye and knew what he wanted, mainly quiet and safe horses for the dudes to ride. Often, they were also older. He always had a small dog for a companion and sometimes a pet raccoon. They always rode with him in the cab of his pickup.

Jim had another constant companion too. A bottle of whiskey. Everywhere, all the time.

At the auction, Jim saw a nice horse come in the ring. Quiet, good shape too. Well-rounded in the belly. It's always better to bring home a fat horse than a skinny one as it took less feed to fatten it up and save some money too.

Jim brought the horse home and stalled it for a few days to get used to its new home. Things were going well.

One morning, Jim came to the barn to feed and water his horses. He heard some unusual noises from the back stall where the new horse was, nickering and some thrashing around in the straw. Perplexed, he walked back the the stall.

There he found a newborn foal, just up on its feet and still wet from birth. The mother was busy attending to it.

Jim thought he bought a fat gelding. Instead, He bought a mare large bellied with a foal inside. Her mammary glands swollen full of milk he mistook for a gelding!

65

Tutoring in Real Time

I DIDN'T REALLY KNOW her, not very well anyway. I knew she had a horse, and I had cared for it once. Lexi was just out of high school and ready to take classes at our community college when she called.

"I'm thinking of being a vet or maybe a vet tech. Could I come ride with you to see what it's like?"

I'm usually open about students, especially those already committed to go to college. They're more serious.

"Sure. How about Saturday, I've got a bunch of cases left over from the week that I need to finish. Come over around 9 in the morning."

Saturday morning, I was working in the office that was connected to the old barn that served as a clinic. I was making phone calls and setting up appointments. Lexi appeared. "Make yourself comfortable. I've got a few more phone calls to make." She left and went into the barn.

About 15 minutes later, I went to find her because I was ready to leave. She was dusting spider webs from the windows. She had already cleaned a couple stalls and swept the floor. I was surprised and, let's face it, pretty impressed.

She continued to ride around with me on Saturdays, and she continued to do clean up, without my asking. Unusual, wonderful behavior.

I then decided I should hire her. I think I felt a little guilty. After all, she was doing lots of work. I even decided to pay her retroactively from the beginning.

For the next year or so she worked with me part time. She was a wonderful helper in the barn and on the road. She was good at handling animals too, particularly horses.

One day she told me she was going to transfer to another college in the eastern part of the state so she could study agriculture. I wished her well and sent along some money for her schooling.

Lexi stayed in contact while at school and would often visit when back home on vacation.

One afternoon in the spring, she called. "What's going on?" I started the conversation.

She started talking quickly and in hushed tones, "I need your help." I immediately was concerned something bad was happening or had happened.

"What?' I answered rather confused.

Quickly, she explained that she was taking a final in an animal science class and needed an answer to a question. She was temporarily tucked away in a restroom.

"When a dairy cow has a calf and can't get up, what's it called?"

"Milk fever most likely although it could be nerve damage."

"It's milk fever, how do you treat it?"

"Calcium solution IV."

Then she was gone. Cell phones don't click when you hang up.

She must have done well since she on went from there to graduate from one of our big universities.

66

U FO Landing

LAWRENCE LIVED in the bottomlands with his wife. The big river was nearby, less than a mile away. Their kids were grown up and gone. He had a small herd of Shorthorn cattle and also worked at the local mill..

Over the years he had built up a pretty good herd by going to Montana or Colorado and bringing home a good bull for breeding.

His cattle were gentle and good to work with, but his place was terrible. Everything for working his cattle was homemade and poorly done at that. Bedsprings just don't make good corrals or gates and they seemed to be in an abundance on this ranch. Fortunately, his cattle, and their breed too, were very agreeable. It was almost like they understood the makeshift world they lived in. In the end, we got things done by using their easy-going nature and taking lots of time.

There was another part of Lawrence. That was his obsession with UFOs. I think they were more important than family and even his cows. He never stopped talking about UFOs and aliens. This was a truly a big deal to him.

He drove his work mates at the mill crazy with his endless talk and speculation and he drove his neighbor, Curtis, the craziest probably because Curtis was trapped living next door.

One day, Lawrence decided it was time to upgrade his herd and go buy a new bull. He and his wife packed up and drove east to Colorado this time. They drove his pickup and pulled a trailer to haul the new bull back home.

This was as much of a vacation as they would ever have. He had Curtis feed the cows and keep a watch for UFOs, so he didn't have to worry about his ranch and cows.

Curtis, as it turns out, had been waiting for this opportunity. As much as he liked Lawrence and was a good neighbor, the UFO stuff drove him nuts.

A few days after Lawrence and his wife left and Curtis was sure they were well down the road, he put his plan to work. He had been thinking about this for a long time.

In one of Lawrence's far pastures, Curtis took a long piece of twine and marked off a large circle. Maybe it was 100 feet across. Then he sprayed it with Roundup, the grass and weedkiller. In days all the grass had died and turned brown.

A couple weeks later, Lawrence returned with his new bull. He had Curtis come to admire it. And he did, because it was a fine bull.

Then Lawrence asked how things went.

"Well, things went fine." Curtis said. "Except something

strange happened in your far pasture. One night we saw lights out there, really bright and they seemed to move right down to the ground. After a while, they went back up again and disappeared."

"I wasn't sure what was going on, but I didn't go out there either. You might want to go out and check things out."

Curtis may have pulled off one of the best pranks ever, but he gave Lawrence more fuel than ever for his UFO obsession. After that, he never stopped talking about it.

67

Use the Hump

DOWN ALONG THE SMALL RIVER, Virginia ran a small flock of motley sheep and some motley cows as well. She pretty much ignored them.

Above the house and across the road was a nice hillside pasture. There she kept her favorites, her Brahma cows that were big, maybe three quarters of a ton, with their long floppy ears, lots of flappy neck skin, long horns, and a large hump above their shoulders. They were unusual in our part of the world. These are hot weather animals, and all that extra skin is to get rid of heat. It's rarely hot around here and the winters are decidedly cool.

They can be a bit squirrelly to handle too as they are quick to react, jump, flee or turn aggressive. They do tend to be one person animals and Virginia was definitely their person.

One of the cows was lame with a swollen and infected foot. I could even see that from across the pasture.

"She's probably got foot rot, an infection and needs antibiotics," I suggested.

"But how are we going to handle her?" I asked.

"Easy. They come to grain, in fact, they do anything for grain. I'll call them in and put lots of grain in the feeder," she replied.

"Then what?" I asked wondering all where this was going.

"You give her a shot while she's eating."

I had a good long-acting antibiotic injection to use, but sticking a large needle in a free standing cow doesn't work very well. It sounded like a good way to get trampled, kicked or gored. Maybe even killed.

"I think she won't like it and maybe do something bad or dangerous," I replied.

"You shoot her in her hump."

"What? That sounds crazy. How did you hear about that?"

"That what my friends with Brahmas tell me."

I wasn't very reassured by her answer.

I was young, had a family to feed, poor life insurance, but I was doing similar things to survive. Probably unfortunate.

I loaded my syringe, put a really new sharp needle on and walked between the eating cows. They stayed quiet, busy enjoying the grain.

"Keep feeding them," I said.

By then I was standing by her large hump. She stayed quiet as I felt around it to see if she reacted. I even pinched it. She just kept eating.

"OK," I decided, "Either this works, or I get maimed or killed."

I stuck the needle in, she didn't move. I connected the syringe to the needle, she just kept eating. I injected the antibiotics, she stayed still.

I slipped back away from her and the other cows. Everything was fine. The cows never stopped eating.

Eventually the lame cow got better, but I did tell Virginia I would not do that again.

68

─────

Walter's Down Cow

WALTER HAD a few cows that he kept on some land down by the river. The land had been in the family for years. It wasn't a particularly good piece of land. Too boggy. It wasn't enough to make a living on, or even come close. He raised enough to feed himself and his family.

Like many guys, he worked at the local mill.

He had called me about a down cow.

I asked my usual questions.

"Kind of cow?"

"Hereford beef cow."

"With a new calf?"

" Nope, none for two years."

"Alert or depressed?"

"Seems fine and will even eat grain."

At least not an emergency it seemed to me.

I looked over my schedule and told him when I could meet up with him.

Later that afternoon I arrived. It was necessary to walk to the cow because to ground was too soft to drive on. I put together a kit of things I thought I would need and off we walked to the cow.

I examined her, but she seemed pretty normal except for the legs. I couldn't find her legs. She wouldn't budge either.

Finally, I started searching for her legs. I found them after some digging around. Each leg had gone through an unusually soft area, probably an area of peat. She was sitting on her belly and chest with her legs trapped straight below her in the boggy soil.

I told Walter the problem, but he didn't want to believe me. After showing where each leg went below the cow, he understood.

I stayed to help. He brought his very old tractor as close to the cow as we dared. I put a rope around her, and he carefully pulled her to solid ground. She immediately got up and walked off to join the rest of the herd.

69

We Got You Covered

FOR YEARS I worked with our county sheriff and animal control to help with neglect and abuse cases in livestock: horses, cattle, sheep, llamas, even pigs.

In most cases it was neglect caused by ignorance, poverty, personal or family tragedies. Sometimes the owner was just gone, dead, imprisoned, or disappeared. We could normally figure out what to do with the animals which usually meant finding somebody to care and feed the animals. I treated the medical problems. A few would need to be euthanized for humane reasons. They were beyond repair.

Predator attacks were often tragic. They were almost always caused by dogs, and many animals did not survive the attack, or had to be euthanized. Fortunately, these were rare.

True abuse is different. This is a malicious human behavior. This behavior was extremely rare. I'm not sure if I can remember such a situation.

One day a deputy sheriff called and asked me to look at a potentially neglected horse. Apparently, a neighbor had complained. The horse was located in the distant corner of our county and down a long winding road in forested country. You might say it was considered a marginal, or sketchy area. I had worked that area before. It was always best just to come when invited and not surprise anybody.

We agreed to meet at a time and place. I would follow him in my truck.

When I arrived at the meeting spot, I found two sheriff deputies and two cars. This seemed a bit excessive for a supposed neglected horse.

"Stay between us and we'll lead you to the place."

"OK," I replied still wondering about the re-enforcements for this trip.

It took a while to get there. On the right side at the end of the road was a barn. I assumed the horse would be there. There was a house behind it, not far away.

The deputies parked on the left across the road. We all got out of our vehicles. They immediately put on their Kevlar vests and strapped on their pistols. I was getting a bit uneasy, if not really concerned.

"Is there going to be a shoot-out?" I'm not sure if my question was serious or maybe hoping to lighten the situation. Maybe both.

One of the deputies turned and calmly said, "We've got you covered. We're going to the house first. Stay where you are for now."

I did. I got behind a large tree and waited.

It wasn't long before they were back.

"What happened?" I asked.

"He's gone," one of the deputies replied. "We had a warrant for his arrest."

Probably not surprising on this road where there are no secrets and everybody protects each other. He was probably out in the woods hiding behind a tree like I was.

We looked at the horse. It was fine.

70

Wintering Well

FOR MOST STOCK PEOPLE, those that raise cattle and horses mainly, getting their animals through the winter is important. Maybe even more than that.

Sometimes of the year are easy, like summer with a lot of grass and nice weather. Easy living as they say. Spring and fall can be iffy or not. It depends on the weather.

Winter is not easy. It's cold, windy, snowy or rainy depending on where you live. No summer grass to eat. Hopefully the hay or silage is good. And there's enough of it to get through winter until spring comes with its fresh, green, nutritious grass.

A lot of these stock people have horses and sometimes very special ones. Good genetics and worth a lot of money. Sometimes they bring the mares to me for artificial breeding. That allows them to use the best of stallions, anywhere. It makes for some very nice baby horses.

It was spring and Bob just brought his best mare for me to evaluate for artificial breeding. It's typical to exam for this.

Near the end of the exam, Charley shows up his best mare. Naturally, they've known each for years. It's sort of an after-winter reunion.

It's pretty evident Charley has put on quite bit of weight, bellied out they call it.

After they greet with hellos and how you're doing, Bob looks Charley over, mainly at his big belly.

Bob then says, "Charley, I can see you wintered well."

71

Thanks for the Bras

AMY HAD a small herd of Red Angus cattle. Nice animals and usually quiet to work with.

Amy was a big girl, strong and tough as nails. I loved working with her because she was so dependable and she made sure I didn't get hurt which was a possibility with her set up for handling cattle.

Every fall, usually very late when things were getting pretty cold, she would wean the calves. After they had settled into not having mothers anymore, she would gather together the young bulls for me to neuter into docile steers. We did that with a banding technique that is commonly used nowadays.

Her mother cows were big milkers and by late fall the calves were really big, up to 700 pounds. The bulls were the biggest of the group too.

Amy would coax each one into very large box-like structure that also served as a scale for weighing. She would move along side them and squeeze them into submission. Well, sort of anyway. That, and holding their tails allowed me to band them.

That morning it was especially cold. I had my new vet assistant, Madison, helping. Amy got the first bull in and reasonably restrained. Madison handed me the device and a large rubber tube we use. I attached it to the device but could not stretch over the large testicles. It was too cold. I finally quit and told Amy my bands were too cold.

She turned to Madison and said, "Give me a bunch of those bands."

She then promptly stuffed them in her bra. "Give this a few minutes," she said.

A bit later she handed me a toasty band to use. I was almost hesitant, especially considering its source, but continued on. After all, we had work to do. It worked fine and that was obviously the secret.

We quickly finished banding all the bulls after that. A job well done, we all agreed.

I didn't think much about it as we often improvise our way through the day out on farms.

The next morning as I was working in the office, getting the day organized, Madison appeared. She walked up to me and dropped three to four bands on my table. She had a sheepish grim.

"What?" I asked.

"When I got ready for bed last night and was undressing, I found these in my bra."

I had no idea she was stuffing bands too!

72

Wolves in the Neighborhood

IT WAS late in the morning on a quite nice spring day. My assistant, Dan, and I were treating a down cow. She just had calved and had an udder full of milk. Now she needed calcium IV. We put a halter on, tied her head around and started the IV.

We were between a couple sheds full of mink. This was a mink farm. There were lots of other sheds full of mink on this farm as well as some cows they used to keep the grass down between them. This was a common practice.

Then it happened.

A wolf howl. And another. And another. Wolves sound nothing like coyotes that we all know so well. I had been to Alaska and had seen and heard wolves. These were wolves.

I was curious. I handed Dan the IV and said, "Drip it in slowly. I'm going to look around."

A couple sheds later I found them. Maybe a dozen. Standoffish, naturally. The enclosure was, well, ramshackle at best. It was made from old mink cages smashed up and wired together. The wolves were already trying to dig under. Fortunately, they didn't seem threatening nor aggressive.

I went back and we finished treating the cow.

As we were cleaning up, Allen showed up. He was one of the sons, but the wayward one. Too many bad choices about chemical indulgence and somewhat addled as a result

"Tell me about the wolves?" I asked.

They were domestic wolves which means they had been raised for generations in captivity. Of course, that didn't mean they were domesticated, or tame, or safe. They were still wolves.

He was going to raise them and sell the pelts which was a good market somewhere. It sounded repulsive to me.

"Be careful with your pens, they're trying to dig out already. You don't want wolves running loose around here," I said.

Allen didn't really respond to my suggestion. He just nodded. I wasn't really surprised.

It was a while, maybe a couple months, but he called. He had a wolf out. Fortunately, it stayed close to the others, on the outside of the pen. He had bought a dart gun too. Now he needed a drug for darting his wolf, and probably more in the future.

I knew this was going to happen and had been thinking about what to do. I had a good drug that was used in wildlife situations. Unfortunately, it had found its way into human abuse too. Fortunately not too much, so not everybody knew about it.

In those days there weren't all the creative chemists

around like today, so it was not being made on the street, or in backyards, or somebody's kitchen.

I made up several doses for him in syringes, instructed him on how to use it and what to expect. Fortunately, that was all straightforward.

When we were finished, he turned and asked, "What happens if I take this drug?"

I expected this and I had been thinking about how to answer him.

"It will kill you," I answered quickly, and as forcefully as I could.

Over the next several months he had more wolves escape, but he always managed to drug them with his dart gun and return them to their pen. He didn't use the drug on himself either.

Finally, his venture was too much and his family forced him sell the wolves.

73

An Ode to Buddy

BUDDY'S in the back field now. He's probably on his last job, caring for an older Arab mare I recently rescued. Being a companion horse, or a buddy is his job.

Buddy is a mini horse, so quite diminutive. He's around 30 years old, so pretty old too. He, also, has pituitary disorder and bad feet. I would say he's in hospice but still working.

Many years ago, I brought Buddy home to live in my barn as a companion for the occasional sick horse I needed to hospitalize. He was a young horse in those days.

Horses are herd animals, and thus social creatures. They do better with friends. I would often keep him in a stall with a low window cut out so he could stick his head out. That way he could see the world and other horses could see him too. I would also put him in the pasture with horse patients.

Buddy could sometimes be a bit mischievous, like taking a nip at your butt as you walked by.

His first serious job was caring for a sick weanling filly. She wasn't too long separated from her mother and had developed an enteric problem. We hospitalized her, treated her and cured her basic problem but she wasn't thriving, not even close. She moped around and had a bad appetite.

Finally, we put Buddy and the filly in a large pen together. That's what she needed. She started improving quickly and was ready to go home in a week. However, she would have no horse companions at home. So, we sent Buddy along. He stayed with her about two months until she was completely well, adjusted and thriving.

A couple years later a mare across the river died. She left a three-month foal as an orphan. At that age young horses can get along without mother's milk, but they do need a special diet. They need a friend too. That's more than important as it's essential.

So over the foal's owners came with their horse trailer. Buddy hopped right in and off they went back across the river. Buddy spent the whole summer and early fall being the young horse's companion. I'm sure he ate the best feed and bossed the young horse around the whole time.

They brought him back in the fall, job accomplished. He walked out of the horse trailer into my pasture and started grazing. Just like he was never gone.

Over the years he was a buddy to young horses, mares, mares with foals, geldings, even stallions. As they say, everybody needs a friend.

Buddy seemed to take his job without any real interest in the other horses besides just being with them. He seemed pretty unemotional., like it was just a job to him.

Except once. Marla had horses, a bunch of horses that

included a donkey and several minis. A virus started going through her horses. It was an enteric problem, a corona virus of all things. Before we figured it out she brought in one of her sick mini mares, Maggie, to stay with me. Of course, she would have a built-in companion, Buddy. Corona virus in horses is an up and down disease, so it took some time to get her through it.

I put both of them in a little pasture I had for special occasions like this. It was a good place to watch her and hopefully the green grass would stimulate her appetite. Right off the bat, Buddy was pretty solicitous towards Maggie. That was not his normal behavior which is usually as a standoffish companion. Maggie was very cute even from a human perspective. Apparently for Buddy she was just plain beautiful. He fell in love! As Maggie got better, they were inseparable. They grazed nose to nose, rested together and played together. Maggie was the love of Buddy's life. As it turns out, the only one.

He had a couple other talents too.

He helped load horses. If a horse was reluctant to load back in its trailer to go home after a visit, we used Buddy. We would lead him into the trailer first and almost always the recalcitrant horse would follow suit.

I bought a special saddle just for mini horses, cute as a bug that saddle. We would saddle him for grandkids, or preschoolers, or kindergarten kids and lead them around. For many it was their first horse ride. If Buddy got tired of all that, he would just sit down and not move anymore.

My youngest granddaughter, Lily, just adored Buddy. They were just the right size for each other for years. She loved cleaning his feet. He always stood very patiently while she picked up and cleaned each foot.

Then we would saddle him up and lead Buddy and her

around our farm or maybe take a longer trip to our neighbor Margaret's farm, Those two spent a lot of time together over the years.

When he was young, he had another trick. I thought he was being mischievous at the time. When I was out repairing a fence, or something like that, he liked to steal my tools, like my fencing pliers. Since I couldn't do much without them, I had to chase him down. I was never able to catch him until I bribed him with a can of grain.

Now I think he wasn't being mischievous but calculating.

ABOUT THE AUTHOR

Russel Hunter DVM was born and raised in Southern California. He attended veterinary school at the University of California at Davis, and graduated in 1965.

He practiced as a country veterinarian in the San Joaquin Valley and the North Coast in California, before settling near Astoria, Oregon, for the next 50 years.

www.ingramcontent.com/pod-product-compliance
Lightning Source LLC
Chambersburg PA
CBHW051823040426
42447CB00006B/344